SpringerBriefs in Energy

SpringerBriefs in Energy presents concise summaries of cutting-edge research and practical applications in all aspects of Energy. Featuring compact volumes of 50–125 pages, the series covers a range of content from professional to academic. Typical topics might include:

- A snapshot of a hot or emerging topic
- A contextual literature review
- A timely report of state-of-the art analytical techniques
- An in-depth case study
- A presentation of core concepts that students must understand in order to make independent contributions.

Briefs allow authors to present their ideas and readers to absorb them with minimal time investment.

Briefs will be published as part of Springer's eBook collection, with millions of users worldwide. In addition, Briefs will be available for individual print and electronic purchase. Briefs are characterized by fast, global electronic dissemination, standard publishing contracts, easy-to-use manuscript preparation and formatting guidelines, and expedited production schedules. We aim for publication 8–12 weeks after acceptance.

Both solicited and unsolicited manuscripts are considered for publication in this series. Briefs can also arise from the scale up of a planned chapter. Instead of simply contributing to an edited volume, the author gets an authored book with the space necessary to provide more data, fundamentals and background on the subject, methodology, future outlook, etc.

SpringerBriefs in Energy contains a distinct subseries focusing on Energy Analysis and edited by Charles Hall, State University of New York. Books for this subseries will emphasize quantitative accounting of energy use and availability, including the potential and limitations of new technologies in terms of energy returned on energy invested.

More information about this series at http://www.springer.com/series/8903

Manfred Hafner · Simone Tagliapietra
Lucia de Strasser

Energy in Africa

Challenges and Opportunities

 Springer Open

Manfred Hafner
Fondazione Eni Enrico Mattei
Milan, Italy

Lucia de Strasser
Fondazione Eni Enrico Mattei
Milan, Italy

Simone Tagliapietra
Fondazione Eni Enrico Mattei
Milan, Italy

ISSN 2191-5520   ISSN 2191-5539   (electronic)
SpringerBriefs in Energy
ISBN 978-3-319-92218-8   ISBN 978-3-319-92219-5   (eBook)
https://doi.org/10.1007/978-3-319-92219-5

Library of Congress Control Number: 2018949331

This Springer imprint is published by the registered company Springer Nature Switzerland AG
The registered company address is: Gewerbestrasse 11, 6330 Cham, Switzerland

Foreword

Access to energy remains a major developmental challenge for the African continent. Recent estimates suggest that about 600 million people or above lack access to electricity. More than 700 million people cook with traditional biomass. Sustainable Development Goal 7 that targets affordable and clean energy therefore speaks to a very important challenge that faces the African continent, especially sub-Saharan Africa.

There is a wide recognition regionally and globally that this challenge needs to be addressed with some urgency. The African Development Bank (AfDB) has, for instance, identified access to energy as one of its High 5 s—that is, one of the five areas that must receive priority as it rolls out its development strategy for the subcontinent. The energy sector has also been identified to be of high importance by an overwhelming number of countries through their nationally determined contributions, as per their commitment to the Paris Agreement. Improving access to energy does not only lead to a reduction of indoor pollution. There are other benefits that include improved educational outcomes (school children will have access to lighting to study), improved health (through the possibility of storing medicines in refrigerators) and potential reduction in rural–urban migration.

The timing of the publication of *Energy in Africa: Challenges and Opportunities* is right. The book pays particular attention to the mix of technologies that would be needed to address energy poverty in the subcontinent. The technologies include those harnessed from both renewable and non-renewable sources. The huge potential from the renewables and opportunities for mixed technologies that do not exclude traditional fuels have been highlighted. The five chapters of this book certainly tackle the major challenges and opportunities in Africa related to access to energy.

There is no doubt that this book makes very useful contributions to our understanding of the ways to address energy access challenges in sub-Saharan Africa. The specific appeal to national governments, foreign investors and the international community to make substantial investments and to commit to making the energy sector effective and efficient is noteworthy. The thinking reflected in this book reinforces previous and emerging knowledge and strategies to address access to clean energy in Africa. Notwithstanding, there is still an avenue to further the debate and the analysis to place energy access in a much broader sustainable development context, especially with respect to expanded electrification goals.

This book pursues an important journey. A critical look is still needed on the institutional and policy frameworks that shape the energy sector. Of particular interest would be how to reform the institutions involved in the generation and distribution of energy. In the same vein, a better understanding of how energy policies in countries with low energy access can address the energy poverty challenge will provide useful insights. The governance of the energy sector needs to be viewed within the context of the sector's value chain. This is particularly significant as the value chain involves multiple players over multiple scales.

It is my hope that this book provides some food for thought for researchers, development agencies, policy makers, bilateral and multilateral partners, and the private sector on the opportunities to ensure access to affordable and clean energy to poor households of the African continent. The insights from the book should be understood in the context that country and regional specificities exist.

Accra, Ghana   Elias T. Ayuk
                                                                                             Director
                                                            United Nations University Institute
                                                                    for Natural Resources in Africa

Acknowledgements

The authors gratefully acknowledge the support of Fondazione Eni Enrico Mattei (FEEM) in realizing this book. A special thanks go to Giacomo Falchetta for his assistance in the development of GIS maps and Barbara Racah for her precious help with the editing process.

Contents

About the Fondazione Eni Enrico Mattei (FEEM)

The Fondazione Eni Enrico Mattei (FEEM), founded in 1989, is a non-profit, policy-oriented, international research centre and a think tank producing high-quality, innovative, interdisciplinary and scientifically sound research on sustainable development. It contributes to the quality of decision-making in public and private spheres through analytical studies, policy advice, scientific dissemination and high-level education. Thanks to its international network, FEEM integrates its research and dissemination activities with those of the best academic institutions and think tanks around the world.

About FEEM's Energy Scenarios and Policy (ESP) Research Programme

The ESP research programme aims to carry out interdisciplinary, scientifically sound, prospective and policy-oriented applied research, targeted at political and business decision makers. This aim is achieved through an integrated quantitative and qualitative analysis of energy scenarios and policies. This innovative and interdisciplinary approach puts together the major factors driving the change in global energy dynamics (i.e. technology, economy, geopolitics and sociological aspects). The ESP programme applies this methodology to a wide range of issues (energy demand and supply, infrastructures, financing, market analyses, socio-economic impacts of energy policies) that are explored from economic, geopolitical and institutional perspectives.

About the Authors

Manfred Hafner is the Coordinator of the "Energy: Scenarios and Policy" research programme at FEEM. He is also Professor of International Energy Studies, teaching at the Johns Hopkins University School of Advanced International Studies (SAIS Europe) and at the Sciences Po Paris School of International Affairs (PSIA). He has 30 years of experience in consulting governments and industry on international energy issues.

Simone Tagliapietra is a Senior Researcher at the "Energy: Scenarios and Policy" research programme at FEEM. He is also Adjunct Professor of Global Energy at the Johns Hopkins University School of Advanced International Studies (SAIS Europe) and Research Fellow at Bruegel, the European economic think-tank. Expert in international energy issues, he also conducted research at the Istanbul Policy Center at Sabanci University and at the United Nations Economic Commission for Europe. He obtained his Ph.D. at the Università Cattolica del Sacro Cuore.

Lucia de Strasser is a Researcher at the "Energy: Scenarios and Policy" research programme at FEEM, where she focuses on the energy transition in sub-Saharan Africa. She has a specific interest in the links between energy policy and environmental management. As a Consultant for the Water Convention of the United Nations Economic Commission for Europe, she uses the water–energy–food nexus approach to improve cooperation in transboundary river basins.

Abstract

Energy poverty is a major barrier to development, and this problem is particularly evident in sub-Saharan Africa, where the majority of the population lives without access to electricity and clean cooking. The continent has more than enough resources to satisfy its current and future demands, but most countries struggle with significant difficulties to attract large investments and to support virtuous small businesses, both necessary to run the race towards universal access to modern energy.

After introducing the problem in its most critical features, this book looks at existing opportunities, with the double objective of providing a snapshot of Africa's resources (both renewable and non-renewable) and to discuss their potential in the light of today's global energy landscape. While the main focus is on the specific challenges of sub-Saharan Africa, when it comes to resources an effort is made to paint a complete picture of the continent, implicitly suggesting the potential for a pan-African energy future.

In the final chapter, the book sheds light on the level of investments required to scale up Africa's energy systems, discussing the role of international financing institutions and calling for greater coordination among European initiatives on the one hand and more effort to tackle the problem of clean cooking on the other hand.

Introduction

Africa is on the move. Since 2000, the continent has seen rapid economic growth (with real GDP growth rates outperforming other major regional economic blocs), improving social conditions (with falling infant mortality rates and rising life expectancies) and progressive political liberalization (if in the 1990s only about 5% of African nations were considered to be democracies, today only a handful of the 55 African states do not have a multiparty constitutional system).

In this context, making energy—and notably electricity—reliable and widely affordable for the population has been and continues to be a key challenge, particularly for sub-Saharan Africa. In energy terms, Africa can be divided into three different regions (Fig. 1). North Africa is almost entirely electrified, and most households also have access to clean cooking. The situation is similar in South Africa (the country), which is predominantly electrified. In the rest of sub-Saharan Africa (SSA) however, most people have no access to power (600 million) and still rely on solid biomass (wood and organic waste) for cooking (780 million).

Notably, two-thirds of SSA's population do not have access to power, while the remaining one-third cannot consume as it would like, due to regular blackouts and brownouts resulting from structural constraints of the available power supply. Given this peculiar situation, this book mainly focuses on energy issues in SSA, where the situation is the most dramatic.

In the SSA region, efforts to promote energy access are gaining momentum, but they are outpaced by population growth. Cities constantly grow with very little urban planning, while villages are scattered over large areas with little or no real infrastructural connection. In this context, reaching universal energy access becomes a real race against time.

Notwithstanding the importance and size of these challenges, Africa's energy sector remains one of the most poorly understood parts of the global energy system. In this context, this book aims at contributing to the understanding of Africa's current and future energy challenges and opportunities.

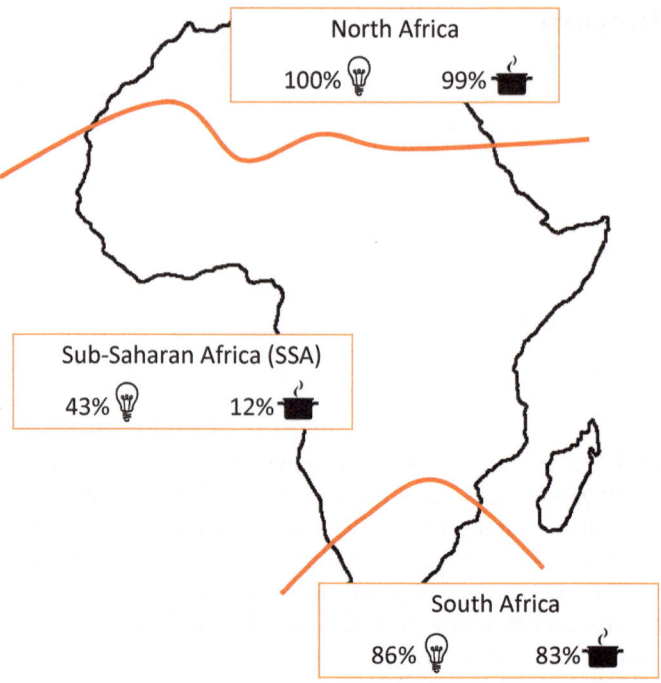

Fig. 1 Three zones of access to electricity and clean cooking. *Source* author's elaboration on IEA, Energy Access database, accessed November 2017

The book develops along four chapters. Chapter 1 analyses the current status of Africa's access to modern energy and points at some key challenges on the way to universal access. Chapter 2 focuses on Africa's hydrocarbon resources and infrastructure and proposes a long-term perspective on their development. Chapter 3 focuses on Africa's renewable energy potential and the actions needed to best value it. Chapter 4 analyses the investments required to scale up Africa's energy systems, sheds light on the key barriers hindering them, and elaborates on potential solutions.

Chapter 1
The Challenge of Energy Access in Africa

Abstract There are multiple dimensions to the problem of energy access in Sub-Saharan Africa, where large shares of population lack a reliable supply of electricity and affordable modern cooking fuels: from insufficient power generation capacity, to difficulties in managing energy infrastructure and attract investments in the sector, to challenges in serving low-income users. Booming populations, urbanization, and ambitions of economic development will all demand more energy. This chapter illustrates the main challenges ahead towards the sustainable development objective of achieving universal access to electricity and clean cooking in the region.

1.1 Today's Landscape

1.1.1 Energy Demand, People and Sectors

Energy—or, more precisely, access to energy—represents one of Africa's greatest obstacles to social and economic development. Few indicators are sufficient to draw a picture of a continent where the energy sector is dramatically underdeveloped, at a time when growing populations and prospects of economic growth would require more energy.

Energy use per capita in SSA[1] is equivalent to one-third of the world's average and one fourth of Middle East and North Africa's (MENA) (Fig. 1.1). Only South Africa's per capita energy use exceeds the world average, and all across SSA there are large disparities in per capita consumption between urban and rural areas, with those in cities typically enjoying better access to modern forms of energy than the others.

---

[1] Throughout the book, "SSA" will be used to refer to the Sub-Saharan region excluding the Republic of South Africa; we will refer to the "subcontinent" to indicate the whole region.

© The Author(s) 2018
M. Hafner et al., *Energy in Africa*, SpringerBriefs in Energy,
https://doi.org/10.1007/978-3-319-92219-5_1

1

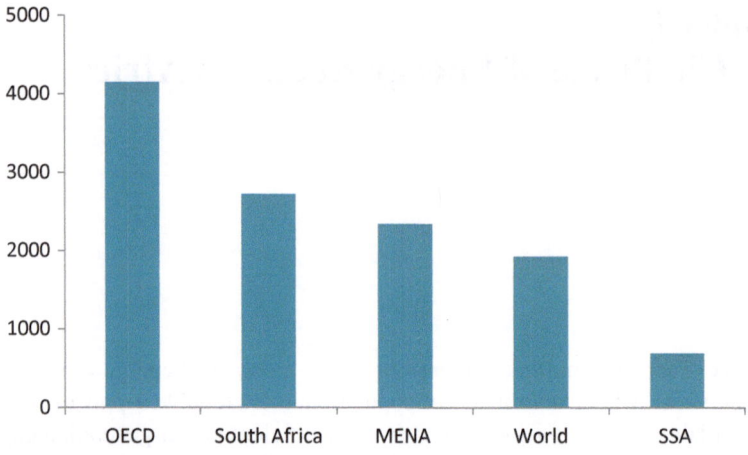

Fig. 1.1 Energy use (kg of oil equivalent) per capita (2014). *Source* World Bank, World Development Indicators, accessed in November 2017

When it comes to electricity,[2] the average person living in SSA consumes as little as 200 kWh/year, against 1,442 kWh in North African countries and 4,148 kWh in South Africa (Table 1.1). The situation is even worse in rural areas, where people can consume as little as 50 kWh/year, a quantity that allows to charge one mobile phone and use minimal lighting for a limited amount of hours a day (International Energy Agency 2014). In perspective, the average citizen consumes in one year considerably less electricity than what a fridge does over the same period of time in the US (Fig. 1.2).

Looking at the whole energy system, it is in the residential sector that lies the core of primary energy consumption. This means two things. Firstly, that more productive sectors like industry and transport consume little amounts of energy (not only if compared to OECD countries, but also to other developing regions). Secondly, that energy consumption is driven by traditional uses: it is solid biomass for cooking that constitutes the bulk (80%) of residential consumption. A global perspective can help visualising the entity of the problem: there are 25 countries in the world today where 90% of the population uses solid biomass for cooking, and 20 of them are located in SSA (International Energy Agency 2017).

The transport sector consumes only 11% of the total primary energy, and productive uses a mere 21% altogether (productive uses include industry, services, and agriculture in order of magnitude of consumption) (International Energy Agency 2014). This reflects a deep infrastructural gap: the penetration of railways, paved roads, and even ports is very low, as is the diffusion of energy (power, hydrocarbons) distribution systems. The implications of this infrastructural under-development include low human mobility and low accessibility of goods (including among others, fuels

---

[2]"Power" will be frequently used as a synonym of "electricity" throughout the book.

Table 1.1 Power consumption per capita in selected African countries

Country or Region	Consumption per capita (kWh/capita)
North Africa	1,442
SSA	200
Angola	346
Democratic Republic of Congo	94
Ethiopia	85
Ghana	320
Kenya	168
Mozambique	507
Nigeria	144
Tanzania	98
Zimbabwe	510
South Africa	4,148
World—High income countries	9,086
World—Low and middle income countries	1,933

Source IEA, World Energy Statistics, 2017 and World Bank, World Development Indicator database, accessed in November 2017

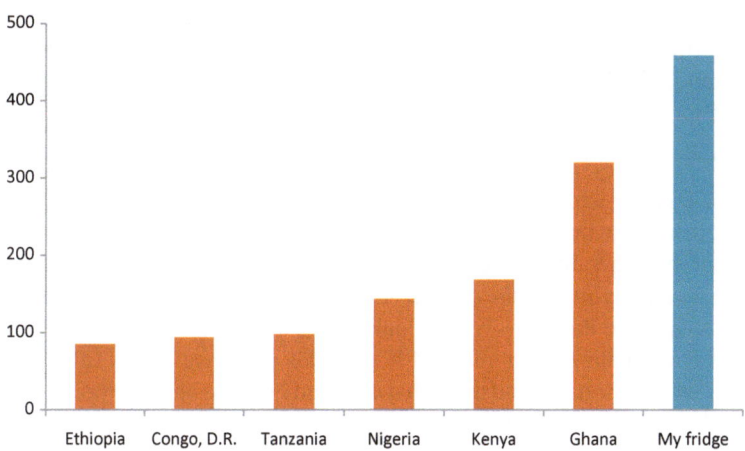

Fig. 1.2 My fridge uses *five* times more energy than the average Ethiopian citizen (kWh) (2015). *Source* author's update of a graphic from (Moss 2013) "My fridge uses nine times more energy than the average Ethiopian citizen" with data from IEA, World Energy Statistics, 2017

and energy equipment), which in turn explains the low levels of productive energy use and the high reliance on biomass.

In SSA the share of electricity in total energy consumption is as low as 4% (against the 19% of North Africa). Mostly, electricity is consumed to power two key industrial activities: mining and refining, and the rest is more or less equally distributed between services and the residential sector.

To a certain extent, small businesses like carpentry or tailoring can get by with little or no electricity, but of course scaling them up becomes impossible without a reliable source of power. In other words, without electricity it is impossible to set up an industrial activity. As electrification tends to develop around the supply of centres of demand that can function as anchor loads for the benefit of surrounding communities, the small consumption of productive sectors is clearly a missed opportunity for broader electrification.

1.1.2 Mapping Access to Modern Energy

From the perspective of modern energy access (Box 1.1) the African continent can be roughly divided into three areas (Fig. 1.3), the most critical situation of access to electricity being in SSA where only 43% of the regional population have access to it. SSA's electrification problem is the most dramatic in rural areas, where electrification rates average at 25%, against 99% in North African countries and 83% in South Africa (Table 1.2).

Box 1.1 Defining and Measuring Energy Access

While there is no universally accepted definition of "energy access", this concept can be generally defined as the *ability of the end user to utilize energy supply that is usable for the desired energy services* (Energy Sector Management Assistance Program, World Bank 2015). The easiest way of measuring access is estimating the number of households that have access to electrical supply on the one hand, and those that use solid biomass and traditional means of cooking on the other, on the basis of available sources such as international statistics, governmental agencies and multilateral development banks. This is, for instance, the approach of the International Energy Agency that—for the purpose of modelling—defines "modern energy access" as the situation of *a household having reliable and affordable access to clean cooking facilities and to a minimum level of electricity consumption which is increasing over time*. This definition does not include "community" access, meaning public services (e.g. street lighting, hospitals) and productive uses (e.g. industry and agriculture).

In order to come up with a sophisticated indicator of energy access it is necessary expand the concept of household access to electricity and clean cook-

---

ing to consider (1) the quality of supply (availability, affordability, adequacy, convenience, reliability) and (2) non-residential sectors of consumption. It is on this basis that the World Bank and other agencies proposed a "multi-tier framework" to measure energy access (Energy Sector Management Assistance Program, World Bank and International Energy Agency 2013). Such framework aims at providing a much clearer picture of access to modern energy by including an indication of both its quantity and quality of supply.

The downside is that populating such framework with real data is a challenging and resource intensive exercise (to give an example, the World Bank is the only source that carries out standardized surveys to enterprises in developing countries on the quality of supply (World Bank)), however progress is being made both in terms of methodologies and data gathering. Digital technologies in particular can allow for the collection of real-time, highly disaggregated data on electricity use on large scales. The manipulation of big data through advanced analytics can produce useful insights on consumption patterns, key for business developers (Onyeji-Nwogu et al. 2017; Ekekwe 2017). In the future, this type of innovation in collecting and manipulating digital data can therefore play a central role in the process of advancing modern energy access.

The number of people in SSA living without access to electricity is also on the rise, as ongoing electrification efforts are generally outpaced by rapid population growth. This trend is here to stay given that SSA population is projected to more than

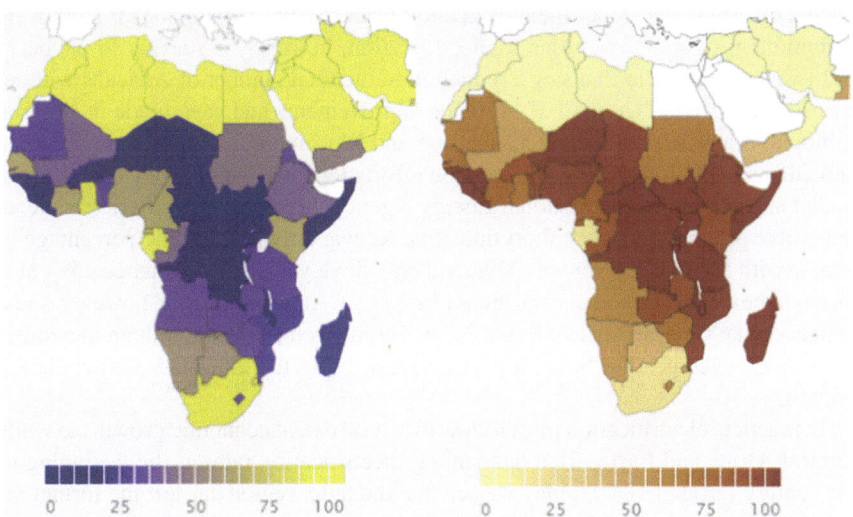

Fig. 1.3 Share of population with access to electricity (left, 2015) and share of population without access to clean cooking (right, 2015). *Source* IEA, 2017, Map © Natural Earth. Energy Access database, accessed in March 2018

Table 1.2 Electrification rates in the three African regions, with a zoom on selected countries (2016)

	National electrification rate (%)	Urban electrification rate (%)	Rural electrification rate (%)
North Africa	100	100	99
SSA	43	71	25
Angola	35	69	6
Burkina Faso	20	58	1
Burundi	10	35	6
Central African Republic	3	5	1
Democratic Republic of Congo	15	35	0
Ethiopia	45	85	29
Guinea	20	46	1
Kenya	65	78	60
Mozambique	29	57	15
Namibia	56	78	34
Nigeria	61	86	34
Rwanda	30	72	12
South Africa	86	87	83

Source IEA, Energy Access database, accessed in November 2017

double by 2050 (UN Department of Economic and Social Affairs 2017). The strong commitment of some countries to electrification, however, is starting to payback: 2014 was the first year that saw a reduction in the total number of Africans without access to electricity. Up until 2014 major improvements had been made in Nigeria, Ethiopia, South Africa, Ghana, Cameroon and Mozambique. Afterwards, Ethiopia and Ghana kept on leading electrification efforts together with Ivory Coast, Kenya, Sudan and Tanzania (International Energy Agency 2017). Some countries made an incredible progress in a very short time, like Kenya: only in 2013, the percentage of people with access to power was 27%, and only three years later it reached 65%, also through the electrification of rural areas (Table 1.2). At the same time, however, some countries like Central African Republic or Burundi remain stuck with an incredibly low power coverage: they have seen no progress, or just too little vis-à-vis population growth.

In practice, electrification rates follow to a good extent economic growth, so while Central Africa and East Africa had similar electrification rates at the beginning of the century (around 10%), today we see that the latter region has left the former far behind. Indeed, no country in Central Africa saw a comparable growth to that of Ethiopia or Kenya.

Country differences in terms of access to modern cooking are relatively less pronounced. In most countries of SSA over 50% of the population relies on solid biomass, and in half of them the share exceeds 90%, with the five most populous countries in the region (Nigeria, Ethiopia, Democratic Republic of Congo, Tanzania and Kenya) bearing the heaviest burden in terms of total biomass consumption.

It can be observed how the three zones of energy access of Fig. 1.3 overlap with three zones that had different historical developments also due to fossil fuels endowment. South Africa could count on massive reserves of coal on which it still largely relies, while the region of North Africa is overall rich in oil and gas. Over time, several countries in SSA entered the ranks of top global producers of fossil fuels too (notably Nigeria and Angola) but their production has been mostly developed for export, with little improvements in terms of universal access to energy and the development of domestic energy markets (Chap. 3). To give a sense of this disparity: South Africa with a population of 57 million has 48 GW of power capacity installed, Egypt with a population of 100 million has an installed capacity of 39 GW, while Nigeria with a population of 195 million is still at 13 GW (Climatescope 2017).

1.1.3 Primary Energy and the Role of Traditional Biomass

Given the lack of alternatives, many in SSA still rely on traditional forms of energy. When looking at the primary energy supply (PES) mix of African regions, it is immediately clear that bioenergy dominates (60–80%) on any other source in SSA (Fig. 1.4). This is in contrast with South Africa and North Africa, where the biggest part of the energy supply (90–99%) comes from fossil fuels—notably from coal in South Africa and from oil and gas in North Africa. After bioenergy, oil is the second most utilized source of energy; then come hydropower and natural gas, the latter concentrated in West Africa. The presence of modern renewables (e.g. solar, wind, geothermal) is still quite limited.

Of course, the regional distribution of energy supply changes considerably in relation to bioenergy. If we exclude it from the account—as it is often done in energy statistics—the cumulative share of North Africa and South Africa in the total primary energy supply of the continent jumps from less than half to three fourth, while the rest of the continent (West, East, Central, and Southern) ends up with one fourth all together (Fig. 1.5).

It should be noted that in the African context "bioenergy" does not refer to modern uses of biomass (e.g. biomass-to-power), instead it refers almost entirely to traditional uses, most notably for cooking purposes (solid biomass fuelled cookstoves, (Chap. 4). Fuelwood, charcoal, and dung are the preferred sources of biomass, particularly where the availability of alternatives is limited or there is a problem of affordability (Lambe et al. 2015).

The massive human, environmental, and in turn economic costs of this underdevelopment are becoming clearer by the day. Indoor air pollution caused by the inefficient use of solid biomass for cooking kills around 600 thousand people every

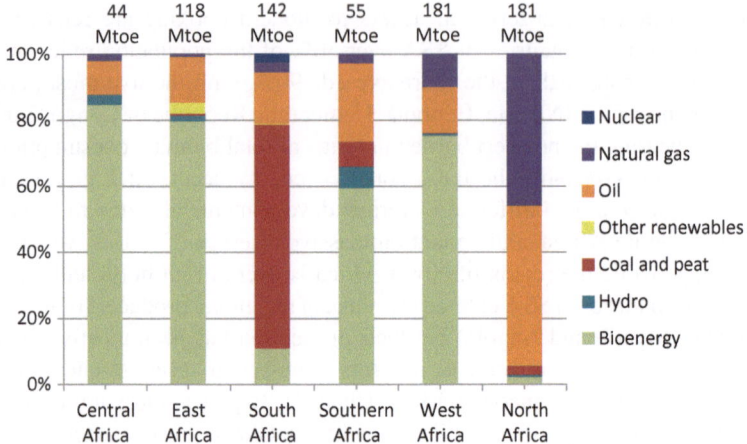

Fig. 1.4 Primary energy supply by region and source, 2015. *Source* Authors' elaboration on OECD database, accessed in November 2017. Note that the averages were calculated on the country data available (i.e. the aggregated value of "other countries" was not taken into account)

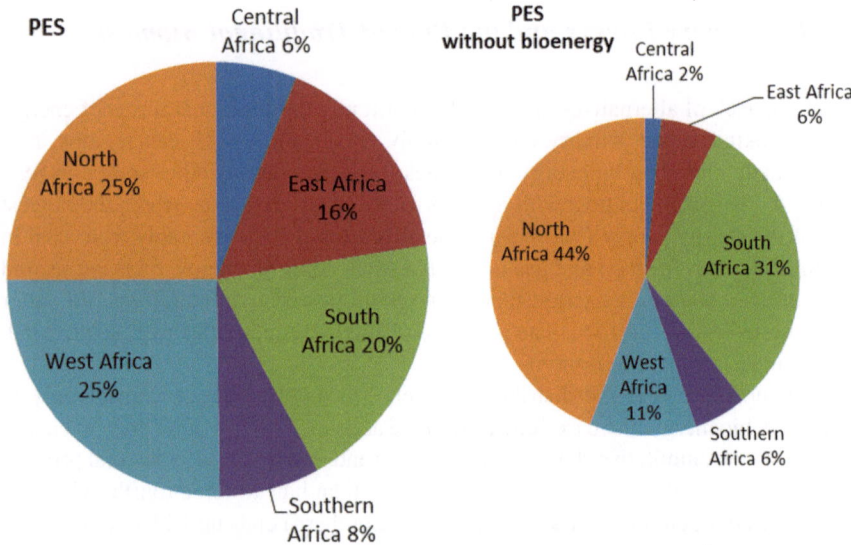

Fig. 1.5 Primary energy supply (PES) by region—including and excluding bioenergy, 2015. *Source* authors' elaboration on OECD database, accessed in November 2017

year, and as population increases this number follows (Africa Progress Panel 2015). Women and young children are the most affected by air pollution because they spend the longest time next to the stove while food is being cooked. Also, women and girls are often those in charge of household management and this includes the collection of water and energy. All in all, they can spend several hours a day fetching water and fuelwood and preparing food, tasks that keep them out of school or employment, and ultimately contribute to hinder women empowerment, and socio-economic development that it would bring.

Of course, apart from the lack of alternatives, free or very cheap fuel is simply more appealing to low income users: fuelwood can be directly harvested or bought for a cheap price in local markets, while agricultural waste is produced at home, or in farm. Typically, even in the event that the price of charcoal and firewood increases, other alternatives remain more expensive.

This problem concerns not only rural populations: worryingly, biomass holds a significant share in cities as well, where other fuels are more accessible. Charcoal is in many cases a more convenient choice than fuelwood for urban households because it is more accessible far from forests: it has a higher energy content, and it is easier to transport and commercialise. In fact, around 80% of urban households in SSA use charcoal (Lambe et al. 2015). It should be noted that charcoal is often a product of fuelwood, and its production process can be highly inefficient. In this context, the penetration of fossil fuel based cooking (with e.g. liquefied petroleum gas (LPG) or kerosene) is limited, and their use is largely concentrated in a few countries: Nigeria, Kenya and South Africa (International Energy Agency 2014).

1.1.4 Quality of Power Supply

The problem of low and intermittent access to electricity is an issue all over SSA. While there is clearly an infrastructural problem, especially in rural areas, of inadequate generation capacity and limited reach of transmission and distribution lines, in many cases even where infrastructure is in place, power supply is either insufficient or unreliable. This is due to several factors like droughts affecting hydropower production, poor maintenance of infrastructure, lack of reliable fuel supply and insufficient transmission and distribution capacity. To give a sense of the magnitude of these problems:

- In SSA power is reported to be unavailable for about 540 h per year on average (International Energy Agency 2014);
- The average efficiency of coal fired power plants in SSA is 34%, (prevalence of sub-critical plants) while that of natural gas fired power plants is 38% (prevalence of open-cycle turbines) (International Energy Agency 2014);
- Losses in power transmission and distribution (including technical losses and thievery) stand at 12% in average across SSA. The problem is tangible in some countries including Nigeria (16%) and Ghana (23%), extremely serious in others such as

Congo (45%), and Togo (73%: the highest in the world). For comparison, average losses are 6% in the OECD area (World Bank).

As already mentioned, the average household consumes little electricity and in general those who have access to the grid may receive electricity only at certain times and in little amounts. It is common that connections are informal or illegal, as many cannot afford to pay for electricity, resulting in missed revenues on the side of power suppliers. Without reliable buyers, the business of producing electricity is not a remunerative one, and of course the final user is the one who sees electricity bills increase, reaching among the highest prices of power per kWh in the world.

Society sees the impact of unreliable supply in everyday life. Unreliable supply not only affects private households, but also public spaces and buildings such as schools and hospitals. Today only 40% of health facilities have access to electricity, and just 28% enjoy a reliable service (International Energy Agency 2017). The impact of an unreliable supply limits the possibility to ensure continuity in medical operations, the storage of vaccines, and in general most activities that are essential in modern hospitals; when public lighting goes off, roads turn to darkness and unsafe; as long the use of computers is limited, the work in public offices remains inefficient; and so on.

Poor supply (low accessibility, high costs, shortages etc.) is a major constraint for industrial activities and businesses in general, as unequivocally confirmed by a survey of the World Bank (Table 1.3). In these conditions most firms have to rely on back-up generators, usually fuelled with diesel. The use of generators can significantly add to the costs of businesses and, unless fuel is subsidised, an increase in international oil prices can make it very expensive. It is clear that a situation of frequent and prolonged power outages can result in major losses and entrepreneurs can be simply held back from embarking in industrial activities.

The agricultural sector uses little amounts of energy as well. Since energy is a key input at all stages of the food value chain—from production (e.g. irrigation, use of fertilizers), processing, storage, and transport—low consumptions generally means low productivity levels (Food and Agriculture Organization 1995). The fact that agriculture generally consumes lower amounts of energy than other productive sectors should not lead to the conclusion that the situation in Africa is simply a reflection of a global trend. Given the weight of subsistence agriculture, a bad agricultural season can knock down entire economies and quickly trigger humanitarian crises. In this picture, low energy consumption in agriculture means low resilience of the sector to weather stress and high vulnerability of entire populations to climate change. The case of Ethiopia is representative: it was a drought in 2016 that put the brakes to an exceptionally fast economic growth rate (International Monetary Fund 2016). This was not an isolated event in Ethiopia, nor in other countries where the economy is still closely linked to rain-fed agriculture (Ali 2012).

Table 1.3 Quality of electrical supply in selected countries (latest available data 2007–2017)

Country	Percent of firms experiencing electrical outages	Average losses due to electrical outages (% of annual sales)	Percent of firms owning or sharing a generator	Percent of firms identifying electricity as a major constraint	How reliable is electricity supply on a scale of 1–7?[a]
Angola	87.7	12.6	79.0	35.7	NA
Democratic Republic of Congo	89.3	7.8	59.5	52.2	2.10
Ethiopia	80.0	6.9	49.1	33.3	3.20
Ghana	89.1	15.8	52.1	61.2	3.10
Kenya	89.4	7.0	57.4	22.2	4.10
Mozambique	51.8	2.4	12.6	24.8	3.00
Nigeria	77.6	15.6	70.7	48.4	1.40
Tanzania	85.8	15.1	43.0	45.8	3.10
Zimbabwe	76.5	6.1	62.3	22.1	3.10
South Africa	44.9	1.6	18.4	20.8	3.90
MENA	57.3	6.6	41	38.6	3.62
World	58.8	4.6	34.1	31	4.71
OECD high income	27.5	0.9	11.4	20.4	NA

Source World Bank, Enterprise Survey, accessed in November 2017 and World Economic Forum, Global Competitiveness Index 2017–2018 (last column)
[a]In terms of lack of interruptions and lack of voltage fluctuations. 1 is highly unreliable and 7 is highly reliable

1.2 Tomorrow's Open Questions

1.2.1 Future Energy Demand

Energy demand is on a steep rise, one of the clearest drivers being population growth. Actually, it would be more appropriate to talk about population boom, especially in East and West Africa. Demographers have been long observing a continued, sometimes accelerated growth with no sign of a reversal in fertility rates. According to UN projections, following these trends by 2100 African population could reach 4.7 billion, which will make up about 40% of the forecasted global population of 11 billion (UN Department of Economic and Social Affairs 2017). Today, Africa is "still" at 1.2 billion (or 16% of global population) but it grows so fast (and urban planning and infrastructure so slow in comparison) that challenges like overcrowding, traffic congestion, pollution, and localised resource depletion are already worrying. In this context, however, the IMF points out that the economic benefits of a very young labour force and urbanization—which should not be underestimated—are yet to be seen (Leke and Barton 2016).

Booming populations and urbanization, industrialization, and expansion of the middle class, will require more energy, however the first two may not necessarily trigger the others, meaning that with no reduction of poverty levels, population may keep on growing and aggregating without a significant increase in actual energy consumption per capita. For what concerns energy, poverty is a major obstacle to the uptake of electricity (at least as long as this remains expensive) and a driver for fuelwood consumption (at least for as long as this remains cheap, or widely available for free). Similarly, low GDPs imply low consumption levels (concentrated in residential sector, for basic activities such as cooking), while higher GDPs mean higher electricity demands with industry, services, transport, and even agriculture playing a more important role as sectors of consumption.

With this in mind, it is clear that future energy demand will largely depend on how countries will perform in terms of economic development. Current trends suggest that some countries will develop more, and faster, than others, and in turn that their energy transition can only happen at different speeds. As of 2017 there is still only one high-income country in the whole continent: the island state of Seychelles (World Bank), but some countries are currently experiencing among the fastest economic growths in the world. In fact, six out of the ten fastest growing economies expected for 2018 are in SSA: Ghana (the highest GDP growth rate globally: 8.3%), Ethiopia (8.2%), Ivory Coast (7.2%), Djibouti (7%), Senegal (6.9%), and Tanzania (6.8%) (World Bank 2018). The landscape is too various to point at common pathways but there are a few facts that stand true for many countries in the continent.

First, agriculture remains a key economic sector for most economies, accounting for around 20% of regional GDP (ranging below 3% in Botswana and South Africa to more than 50% in Chad), a very high share when compared to the global 6%. The sector employs more than 60% of the total labour force and provides livelihoods to many small scale producers in rural areas (African Development Bank et al. 2017). The crop sector dominates the total agricultural production value and, as already mentioned, the sector remains un-modernised and dependent on rain-fed crops making the impact of droughts and climate change, extremely damaging. Examples of how electricity can improve agricultural activities are many and range from the more traditional uses for irrigation and cold storage to the more sophisticated digital applications for real time weather forecasting and resource use monitoring.

Second, mining is the single largest industrial activity in the subcontinent, contributing significantly to fiscal revenues and GDPs. For instance in Burkina Faso, the Democratic Republic of Congo, Guinea, Mauritania, Mozambique, and Zambia the sector accounts for more than half of total exports. Mining is generally associated with weak direct employment compared to its contribution to GDP and fiscal revenues and yet at least in principle it has the potential for large local impacts that can foster change in local economies (Chuhan-Pole et al. 2017). Reflecting the weight of this sector, electricity demand for mining represents half of the total electricity demand in the region as a whole, while in countries such as Liberia, Guinea, Mozambique, and Sierra Leone it consumes as much as three times the amount of electricity used by the other sectors together (International Energy Agency 2014).

Third, economic growth is being driven more and more by sectors with low energy intensity like the textile industry but also, most notably, agriculture and services (International Energy Agency 2014). Within this group, banking and telecommunication are showing particular vigour, which is expected to bring significant advancement, if not disruption, not only in the energy industry but also in other key sectors, notably agriculture (Bright 2016). In particular, digitalization and the innovative application of "fintech" solutions (to payments, loans, financial advice, and so on), are giving an important boost to local entrepreneurship.

Overall, the IEA estimates that following current demographic and economic trends as well as national energy plans, by 2030 the total primary energy demand in SSA will grow by 30%. Over half of this energy will be demanded in the form of traditional biomass, as the number of people without access to clean cooking will remain huge (900 million). This will be followed by oil, to satisfy transport and cooking needs (in the form of LPG and kerosene), and modern renewables. Natural gas demand will be largely concentrated in the countries that have domestic reserves. Demand of coal will triple across the subcontinent but its consumption will decline in South Africa due to stock depletion and fuel substitution (with renewables) (International Energy Agency 2017).

According to the IEA, compared to the recent past there will be at least two extremely important positive changes in SSA energy sector. First, new investments in the electricity sector to satisfy local demands will largely exceed those in the extractive industry for the export of fossil fuels. Second, renewables and PV in particular will lead the growth in power generation capacity satisfying the largest share of additional energy demand in the period 2016–2030. Investments in renewables will be driven more and more by their cost competitiveness, particularly in a scenario of high oil prices.

Of course, while it is typically assumed that SSA will not experience an industrial boom comparable to that of India or China, it is nevertheless possible to picture the impact of massive industrialization on primary energy demand. In this type of scenario, by 2035 Africa's energy demand could be offsetting the reduction in energy consumption of post-industrial China and start driving global growth (British Petroleum 2017).

1.2.2 More Power, for All

Given the central role of electric power in modern society, its cleanness and versatility for a variety of uses, achieving universal access to electricity quickly and cost-effectively can be considered the single most important energy-related objective for African policy makers. The socio-economic benefits of universal access to electricity largely outweigh the costs of achieving it (Fig. 1.6). Moreover, particularly in SSA,

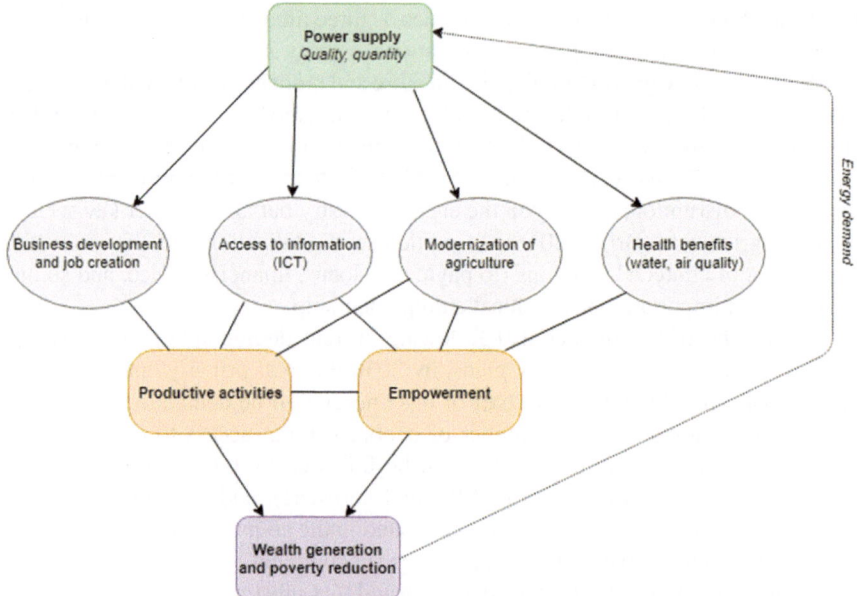

Fig. 1.6 Benefits of electrification. *Source* author's elaboration

the greenhouse gas emissions brought by the increased in power generation would be at least partially offset by the reduction in the traditional use of biomass.

Considering current policies in place, 1 billion people should gain access to electricity in Africa by 2040, but there is a high chance that electrification efforts will be outpaced by population growth. In this case, the number of people without access in 2030 could remain unchanged, if not increase (around 600 million). Taking a global perspective, by then Africa will account for 75% of the world population without access (from 50% today) and the continent will be the last one to be "left behind" in the global electrification process (International Energy Agency 2017).

The race against time to power the African continent will unfold in different ways due to an uneven distribution of resources, however a massive stock of renewables encourages a vision of a low-carbon development for the overall continent (International Energy Agency 2014; International Renewable Energy Agency 2015). It is estimated that the 90% of hydropower potential in the continent is still untapped and a good part of it is concentrated in Central Africa, followed closely by Southern and East Africa. Wind on the other hand is mostly available in the East, West and Southern regions. Geothermal potential is concentrated in the East and South, with Kenya leading the way of technology development. Solar energy, finally, is massive across the whole continent. Indeed, it is expected that solar will play a key role in the energization of most countries, also due to the increasing viability of solar-based mini-grids.

Notably, the uptake of renewable energy is happening less and less because of top down policies driven by sustainability objectives. In fact, the deployment of renewable technologies today is increasingly driven by their cost competitiveness. It seems important to underline how big of a shift this is for the energy sector and what unique opportunity this may be, especially for fossil fuel scarce developing countries. This does not mean that fossil fuels will not play a role, but it looks like they will not dominate the scene alone either (as it happened in the first stages of energy development of all other continents before). Put in a different way, those countries who have fossil fuel resources will most probably want to exploit them and if there is a sufficiently large domestic and/or export market this will make economic sense. However, those countries who will need to import them may still find it expensive or impractical (due to poor infrastructure), but the falling costs of renewables may finally offer a valid alternative.

1.2.3 Grids, Mini-Grids, or Stand-Alone Systems?

With scattered populations and a huge infrastructural gap, electrification will spread as a sort of patchwork. National grids will reach out only as far as it is technically and economically viable, so that remote demand will need to be met otherwise. Essentially, this means building mini-grids that link isolated demand (a mine, a village, an irrigation scheme) with a local source of electricity production (e.g. solar, small hydro) and a back-up generator or a battery that can jump in as needed. New technological progress and the development of ad-hoc business models are making these systems more and more viable, and yet without an anchor load building a mini-grid may just not make economic sense, therefore even a widespread deployment of mini-grids will still leave many off-grid. For them, electrification can be only provided by stand-alone systems, to make at least limited power available to satisfy basic services, such as phone charging and lighting.

Grids, mini-grids and stand-alone systems have very different underpinning economic models even though, technically, at least grids and mini-grids look similar (Fig. 1.7). A grid brings power from a number of centres of production (power plants) to many users through a capillary system of transmission and distribution lines, hence it basically differs from a mini-grid in terms of the amount of power that it carries to users. However, building grids requires huge financial effort (and risk) so that this business is ultimately in the hands of governments and public companies, while mini-grids can be built by private companies, local entrepreneurs, or even cooperatives of users, as long as there is a clear return on investment and an enabling business environment to support them. Stand-alone systems, finally, are typically distributed by private companies to single users. The business model that is proving to be most successful so far in Africa is that of PV modules that users rent and gradually come to own, through Pay As You Go payment schemes.

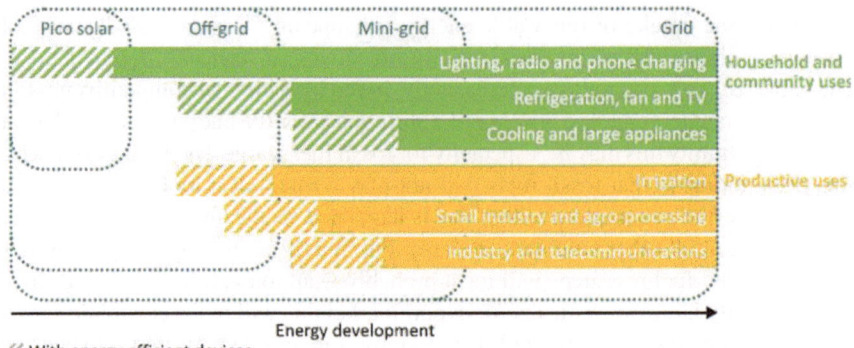

Fig. 1.7 Means of electrification and their possible uses. *Source* © OECD/IEA 2017 World Access Outlook (World Energy Outlook Special Report), IEA Publishing

Now, given the urgency of the problem and the entity of financial gaps, some questions arise. When is it more convenient to build mini-grids and when to extend grids? Where does it make sense to provide stand-alone modules? And even: what is the cost-optimal pathway to reach universal access to electricity (Chap. 5)? These questions point at a need to plan electrification sensibly taking into account real distances, locations of demands, and potential anchor loads (also keeping in mind that future interconnections could end up linking mini-grids that were initially built in isolation).

The relative shares of investment in grids, mini-grids, and stand-alone systems can vary significantly by country, but most policy makers in SSA plan for universal electrification largely in terms of national grid expansion. This should change, as a greater effort to deploy mini-grids and stand-alone solutions will be instrumental and necessary to achieve universal access by 2030. And this will not be an easy task. For instance, diesel prices still determine the viability of mini-grid solutions by affecting the cost of back-up generators (and will keep on doing so as long as storage solutions will be too expensive) (Mentis et al. 2017). Governmental support will be crucial to boost the sector, particularly when it comes to supporting private investors (TFE Consulting 2017).

Clearly, an increased focus on decentralisation should not end up downplaying the role of centralised production and regional interconnections. Big cities and related industrial areas will likely remain the largest share of electricity consumption and for many countries regional interconnections could significantly accelerate universal electrification. At the same time, existing complementarities between different countries' resource bases (particularly wind, hydropower, and natural gas) make regional interconnections a sensible option that also allows for deployment of large scale renewable projects.

At this point it seems important to recall that the challenges of energy access are so various and intertwined, that reaching users does not necessarily guarantee a good quality of supply, nor even it ensures accessibility by the side of low-income users

(Hogarth and Granoff 2015). The latter in particular is the problem of the so-called "under-grids", who cannot afford to pay for electricity hence can use it only when it is subsidised. Ultimately, the viability of grid extension, mini-grid construction and stand-alone system delivery will depend largely on the ability to design appropriate business models. Remarkably, these will need to make electricity affordable for the poorest, exploiting the ability to pay of the most reliable customers, most notably the mining industry (Ghosh Banerjee et al. 2014). In general, future grids (and mini-grids) in SSA will not only need to be "smart", but also "just", meaning that social inclusion needs to be a cornerstone of grid design in the region in order for it to be truly successful (Welsch et al. 2013).

1.2.4 The Changing Role of Fossil Fuels

Importantly for climate change concerns, Africa may be the first continent to develop without coal. While this is a resource that still features in the plans of several countries, and the increasingly prominent role of China in the continent's energy landscape has long anticipated a coal boom (led by China's strong coal industry), recent developments do not reflect such a clear trend. Among fossil fuels, natural gas appears to be a major competitor (Chap. 3), one reason being that natural gas reserves are better distributed across the continent (i.e. Nigeria, Mozambique, Angola, Algeria are all important natural gas producers, whereas the coal industry is virtually concentrated in South Africa). Also, it is a cleaner option than coal—not only in terms of greenhouse gas emissions but also in terms of air pollution. While this has been of relatively little concern for many countries on a development path, the perspective of policy makers may well be changing following increasing evidence that pollution is the first cause of death globally and air pollution sits at the top of the list, even before water contamination (Landrigan et al. 2018).

Oil and gas have a rather significant role to play for the energization of the continent. Unlike coal, their role in the energy system goes beyond power production, and their possible substitution in some key sectors of consumption is still at an early stage. First and foremost, the transport sector still heavily relies on oil (gasoline and diesel) and to some extent natural gas, and while electric cars are starting to emerge as an alternative, at least in developed countries, the use of electricity for subsectors of heavier transport (e.g. cargo ships and aeroplanes) remains impractical with the current storage technology. The demand for natural gas, on the other hand, is also driven by non-energy sectors, most importantly the production of fertilizers of which the agricultural sector in Africa is thirstier by the day given quickly decreasing soil productivity (though it should be noted that the massive use of chemical fertilizers may actually end up worsening the problem of soil degradation).

Another key sector where fossil fuels have a role to play is cooking. Actually, considering the magnitude of the problems of indoor pollution and forest degradation

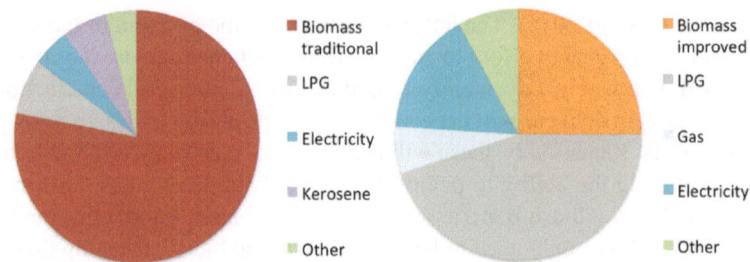

Fig. 1.8 Cooking fuels today (left) and in 2030 in the IEA Energy for All Scenario (right) in SSA. *Source* authors' elaboration on © OECD/IEA 2017 World Access Outlook (World Energy Outlook Special Report), IEA Publishing. *Note* IEA's "Energy for All Scenario" assumes that by 2030 all countries will achieve universal access to clean cooking; "Other" include coal and biogas

in SSA, their uptake as substitutes of fuelwood could be a sensible option. So far, it is largely due to LPG and kerosene that most of the progress has been registered in the sector, not only in Africa but all over the developing world.

1.2.5   The Future of Cooking

More than for electrification, policies aimed at modernizing access to clean cooking have proved so far largely insufficient, and the challenge of achieving universal access to clean cooking still receives less attention than that of electrification. One of the reasons for this is that there has been no real market breakthrough of innovative stand-alone technologies (e.g. solar or biogas cookers) yet, and the alternatives to traditional cooking today are more or less the same we had decades ago, most importantly petroleum based fuels and electricity. In other words, the main challenge of clean cooking remains that of improving the logistics, and increasing the affordability and cultural acceptance of, alternative solutions to rudimentary cookstoves.

Figure 1.8 shows SSA's cooking fuel mix today, compared to a 2030 scenario where everyone has gained access to clean cooking (IEA's "Energy for All Scenario"). This picture is quite far from what is expected to be the outcome of current policies (IEA's "New Policy Scenario"), which are going to leave 900 million people, or 56% of the population, without viable alternatives to solid biomass (International Energy Agency 2017).

Without major improvements to current trends and policy commitments, progress will likely be seen in urban areas only and will not be matched by an overall reduction in the demand of solid biomass, whereas achieving universal access to clean cooking will require a whole new level of commitment (also in financial terms, see Chap. 5).

Providing an alternative to solid biomass for everyone will mean stimulating the use of all available alternatives. As anticipated, fossil fuels and in particular LPG have an important role to play—the IEA estimates that about 90% of those who will shift away from solid biomass by 2030, will move to LPG—however difficulties of distribution will likely remain a major barrier to their wider uptake (Van Leeuwen et al. 2017) (Chap. 3). The effect of electrification can also have a major impact on the way people cook: today, for instance, electricity is already widely used in urban areas in South Africa, and assuming sufficient affordability, it can become a key fuel in the future cooking fuel mix of other countries too.

Modern forms of bioenergy, including the product of biomass residues treatment (e.g. biogas, pellets) and liquid biofuels (i.e. bioethanol and biodiesel) are potentially very promising options, although their theoretical potential is often restricted by a number of factors such as high costs, complexity of fuel production, storage, and transport, or even competition with food production (Chap. 4). Pushing these solutions will require an explicit effort to establish whole new value chains for products coming from agriculture, forestry, and waste management.

Notably, even in this scenario of universal access to clean cooking, efficient and advanced[3] cookstoves ("biomass improved" in the picture) will have a major role to play in SSA. They will likely remain the only feasible upgrading from the status quo for many—especially in rural areas—and, in terms of fuel, charcoal will play an increasingly important role compared to fuelwood and other solid biomass (e.g. agricultural residues). It should be noted that the use of fuelwood is difficult to eradicate even where alternatives are available: it is possible, and indeed common, to own more than one type of stove and fuel ("fuel-stacking") and using one or another depending on fuel availability, price, or even to satisfy food taste preferences.

The benefits of achieving universal access to clean cooking would be immense and would include improvement of health conditions, local job creation, gender empowerment, and reduced forest degradation (and in turn improved climate mitigation at global level).

References

Africa Progress Panel (2015) Africa progress report 2015—Power people planet: seizing Africa's energy and climate opportunities. Geneva

African Development Bank, Organization for Economic Co-operation and Development, United Nations Development Programme (2017) African economic outlook. OECD Publishing, Paris

Ali SN (2012) Climate change and economic growth in a rain-fed economy: how much does rainfall variability cost Ethiopia? Ethiopian economics association working paper

Dright J (2016) A brief overview of Africa's tech industry and 7 predictions for its future. In: World economic forum on Africa. https://www.weforum.org/agenda/2016/05/a-brief-history-of-africa-s-tech-industry-and-7-predictions-for-its-future/. Accessed 2 Nov 2017

British Petroleum (2017) BP energy outlook

Chuhan-Pole P, Dabalen AL, Land BC (2017) Mining in Africa: are local communities better off? Africa development Forum series. The World Bank, Washington, DC

---

[3]In the sense of efficiency of combustion and cleanliness, in particular when it comes to indoor pollution.

Climatescope (2017) Climatescope 2017. In: Climatescope. http://global-climatescope.org/en/resu
    lts/. Accessed 6 Mar 2018
Ekekwe N (2017) How digital technology is changing farming in Africa. Harvard Bus Rev. https://
    hbr.org/2017/05/how-digital-technology-is-changing-farming-in-africa. Accessed 12 Jul 2017
Energy Sector Management Assistance Program, World Bank (2015) Beyond connections: energy
    access redefined. ESMAP technical report 008/15
Energy Sector Management Assistance Program, World Bank, International Energy Agency (2013)
    Global tracking framework
Food and Agriculture Organization (1995) Future energy requirements for Africa's agriculture.
    Chapter 4. Scenarios of energy and agriculture in Africa. http://www.fao.org/docrep/v9766E/v9
    766e05.htm. Accessed 20 Jun 2017
Ghosh Banerjee S, Romo Z, McMahon G, Toledano P, Robinson P, Pérez Arroyo I (2014) The
    power of the mine: a transformative opportunity for Sub-Saharan Africa
Hogarth R, Granoff I (2015) Power generation alone won't deliver energy to Africa's poor. Overseas
    Development Institute. https://www.odi.org/comment/9577-africa-energy-poverty-distribution-e
    lectricity-generation. Accessed 2 Nov 2017
International Energy Agency (2014) Africa energy outlook—a focus on energy prospects in Sub-
    Saharan Africa (World Energy Outlook Special Report)
International Energy Agency (2017) Energy access outlook (World Energy Outlook Special Report)
International Monetary Fund (2016) World economic outlook: Too slow for too long
International Renewable Energy Agency (2015) Africa 2030: roadmap for a renewable energy future
Lambe F, Jürisoo M, Wanjiru H, Senyagwa J (2015) Bringing clean, safe, affordable cooking energy
    to households across Africa: an agenda for action. Background paper to the Africa progress panel
    2015 report Power, people, planet: seizing Africa's energy and climate opportunities. Prepared
    by the Stockholm Environment Institute, Stockholm and Nairobi, for the New Climate Economy.
    People, planet: seizing Africa's energy and climate opportunities
Landrigan P, et al. (2018) The Lancet Commission on pollution and health. The Lancet
    39(110119):462–512. https://www.sciencedirect.com/science/article/pii/S0140673617323450v
Leke A, Barton D (2016) What's the future of economic growth in Africa? In: World economic
    forum on Africa. https://www.weforum.org/agenda/2016/05/what-s-the-future-of-economic-gro
    wth-in-africa/. Accessed 2 Nov 2017
Mentis D, Howells M, Rogner H, Korkovelos A, Arderne C, Zepeda Eduardo, Siyal S, Taliotis C,
    Bazilian M, de Roo A, Tanvez Y, Oudalov Alexandre, Scholtz E (2017) Lighting the World: the
    first application of an open source, spatial electrification tool (OnSSET) on Sub-Saharan Africa.
    Environ Res Lett 12:085003. https://doi.org/10.1088/1748-9326/aa7b29
Moss T (2013) My fridge versus power Africa. In: Center for global development. https://www.cg
    dev.org/blog/my-fridge-versus-power-africa. Accessed 3 Nov 2017
Onyeji-Nwogu I, Bazilian M, Moss T (2017) The digital transformation and disruptive technologies:
    Challenges and solutions for the electricity sector in African markets
TFE Consulting (2017) Kenya: the world's Microgrid lab. Executive summary
UN Department of Economic and Social Affairs (2017) World population prospects—population
    division—United Nations. https://esa.un.org/unpd/wpp/Graphs/Probabilistic/. Accessed 24 Oct
    2017
Van Leeuwen R, Evans A, Hyseni B (2017) Increasing the use of liquefied petroleum gas in cooking
    in developing countries
Welsch M, Bazilian M, Howells M, Divan D, Elzinga D, Strbac G, Jones L, Keane A, Gielen D,
    Balijepalli VSKM, Brew-Hammond A, Yumkella K (2013) Smart and Just Grids for sub-Saharan
    Africa: Exploring options. Renew Sustain Energy Rev 20:336–352. https://doi.org/10.1016/j.rse
    r.2012.11.004
World Bank World Bank Open Data (2017a) http://data.worldbank.org/. Accessed 18 May 2017

World Bank World Bank Country and Lending Groups—World Bank Data Help Desk (2017b) https://datahelpdesk.worldbank.org/knowledgebase/articles/906519. Accessed 24 Oct 2017

World Bank (2018) Global economic prospects, January 2018: broad-based upturn, but for how long?

Chapter 2
The Role of Hydrocarbons in Africa's Energy Mix

Abstract Africa is rich in hydrocarbon resources, with some countries ranking among the biggest exporters in the world. Compared of North Africa and also South Africa, where this endowment translated into the creation of domestic markets, in the rest of Sub-Saharan Africa investments have largely focused on the upstream industry for export. This chapter elaborates on the possible role of hydrocarbon resources in the future of SSA countries, taking into account the new reality that renewable energy is becoming more and more competitive as well as the fact that—despite increasing climate and environmental concerns that see international financing institutions increasingly reticent to support investments in fossil fuels—the sector remains strategic for many countries.

The African continent is richly endowed with hydrocarbon[1] resources, although they are distributed unevenly. With the exclusion of the North African region, oil and gas resources are generally exploited below potential and, where the sector has developed, investments have prioritized extraction for export over the development of domestic markets. In fact, Africa is a net exporter of hydrocarbons and it accounts for 8% of global gas exports and 10% of global oil exports (British Petroleum 2017a). Africa is a sort of frontier continent for oil and gas companies because it is the least explored in terms of resources and at the same time the least developed in terms of infrastructure. Notwithstanding uncertainties, today's estimates indicate that the region has enough oil, gas, and coal to supply its current and future demand on its own (International Energy Agency 2014) but, in most cases, there are obstacles of various nature that prevent countries from fully benefit from their exploitation.

Hydrocarbons already play a big role in the energy mix of African countries—and so does the capacity of resource-rich countries to extract, process, transport, commercialize, trade, and ultimately value them as social assets. Among commercial energy sources, oil, gas and coal indeed constitute the largest part of the African primary energy demand: excluding bioenergy from the account (see Chap. 2) oil accounts

---

[1] "Hydrocarbons" is a broader term than "fossil fuels": the latter refers to the use of the first in the energy sector, however these terms are often used interchangeably, including in this book.

M. Hafner et al., *Energy in Africa*, SpringerBriefs in Energy,
https://doi.org/10.1007/978-3-319-92219-5_2

for 42%, followed by natural gas (28%) and coal (22%). Renewables only constitute 8%, most of which comes from hydropower (British Petroleum 2017a).

As the global energy landscape transforms, so does the role of fossil fuels. The most notable global change is that the primacy of coal as the cheapest fuel for power generation is being challenged by a new competitor: low-cost photovoltaic (International Energy Agency 2017a). Once PV becomes affordable and available, it becomes particularly appealing for African countries because—unlike coal—the sun is available everywhere. This is bringing a whole new perspective on rural electrification (Chap. 4). Still, we are far from seeing fossil fuels becoming subordinate to renewables. As the world energy system evolves, oil remains fundamental for transportation and the petrochemical industry, natural gas becomes strategic all across the energy system (including flexible power generation to back up variable renewables), and coal remains a competitive fuel for baseload power generation for those countries that have easy access to it, or which energy system is already dependent on it. Importantly for SSA, hydrocarbon-based fuels also have an important role to play as an alternative to solid biomass for cooking.

When it comes to the issue of greenhouse gas emissions from the energy sector—a major drawback for the use of fossil fuels at global level—most analysts agree that climate concerns should not put the brakes on the electrification process in Africa, and that universal access to modern energy is in itself a prerequisite for sustainable development. CO_2 emissions from fossil fuel combustion could be at least partially offset by a reduction in the use of solid biomass in households, which causes forest degradation and in turn the ability of forest stocks to act as carbon sinks.[2] The local impact of pollution from hydrocarbons is a more problematic issue. Air pollution from coal-fired production and traffic congestion in cities, potential land and water contamination from oil and gas extraction: these are some environmental and social challenges that African societies will inevitably struggle with when developing fossil fuels, and which will require strong environmental regulations and responsible governance.

This chapter includes a short note on nuclear energy (Box 2.1), covered here only because its primary source (uranium) is a non-renewable one, like hydrocarbons. However nuclear energy is quite different from fossil fuels, and in many ways. While the combustion of fossil fuels is responsible for high emissions of greenhouse gases, nuclear is typically considered a carbon-free source. Also, large scale electricity production is practically the only energy use of uranium (if we exclude military applications), whereas hydrocarbons are versatile resources that can be used directly by final users, hence they are truly ubiquitous throughout the energy system. Finally, the upfront investment cost of nuclear power is much higher than fossil-fuel based options—which is the main reason why it is not expected to play a big role in the African electrification process.

---

[2]It should be noted that there is a huge uncertainty surrounding the actual CO_2 budget of the traditional use of firewood (Bailis et al. 2015), which makes a direct comparison with emissions from fossil fuels a tricky exercise.

Box 2.1 Nuclear Energy

Africa supplies around 18% of the world's uranium demand. All of it comes from the subcontinent and more specifically from Namibia (10%), Niger (7%), and South Africa (1%) (where it is a by-product of gold and copper mining). Previous mining activities in Gabon and Malawi were ceased because decreasing global prices of uranium made its extraction uneconomical. This is also the main reason why production never started in most of the countries that found uranium reserves, even though some of them were particularly rich of it, and highly motivated to begin extraction. Further African countries with known potential are: Algeria, Botswana, Central African Republic, Democratic Republic of Congo, Guinea, Equatorial Guinea, Mali, Mauritania, Morocco, Nigeria, Tanzania, Zambia, and Zimbabwe (World Nuclear Association 2017).

A number of countries are considering to start producing nuclear power but, as of today, the only active nuclear power plant in the continent ("Koeberg") is located in South Africa, where it supplies around 5% of the total power demand. South Africa plans to expand nuclear capacity, and nuclear is one of the technologies that South Africa aims at utilizing in order to reduce its dependency on coal, although recent policies seem to favour small scale, decentralised production over large, capital intensive projects, which ends up slowing down nuclear projects.

Nuclear is one of the most controversial energy sources and typically divides the public opinion. On the one hand, greenhouse gas emissions from nuclear are in the range of solar and wind, even looking at the whole life cycle of a nuclear power plant (although there is considerable uncertainty surrounding nuclear waste disposal, which remains so far unaccounted for in estimates) (Sathaye et al. 2011). On the other, the environmental impact of radioactive waste disposal is one of the main concerns of those who oppose nuclear energy, along with safety concerns, and the risk of nuclear proliferation (about this, it is worth noting that South Africa is the only country in the world that voluntarily dismantled its nuclear weapons, becoming a champion of "peaceful nuclear energy").

In sum, nuclear power is a very expensive technology that requires strong, ad hoc safety and environmental legislation to be in place, and that needs to be coupled with high power transmission capacity. Given the current infrastructural, financial, and governance landscape, now nuclear development in Africa faces significant uncertainty, and for sure it is not imminent (Krikorian and Evrensel 2017).

2.1 Reserves and Producing Countries

Hydrocarbons are the result of the slow transformation of organic material under-ground and underwater, in conditions of low oxygen, high temperatures, and high pressures. The formation of coal is substantially different from that of oil and gas, hence while oil and gas are frequently found in combination, coal deposits are com-pletely unrelated.

When talking about hydrocarbons, there is an important difference to be made between "resources" and "reserves". In order to become reserves, resources need to be carefully assessed in quantity and quality, which takes a significant effort in terms of geological exploration. Also, reserves need to be commercially exploitable, meaning that it has to be possible—and economically sound—to extract the resource using available technology and at market conditions. Reserves can be ranked to various degrees of confidence that they can be recovered (possible, probable, proved). Let us first look at oil and gas reserves and then at coal.

2.1.1 Oil and Gas

A recent geological survey sets the upper bound of Africa's potential at 1,273 billion bbl of oil (including condensate gas from gas extraction) and 82 tcm of natural gas (including associated gas from oil extraction) and estimates that it would be "technically and economically feasible" to recover around 381 billion bbl of oil and 73.8 tcm of gas (Modelevsky and Modelevsky 2016). However, "proved" reserves according to BP are much smaller: 128 billion bbl of oil and 14 tcm of gas. Then, according to the IEA, "remaining recoverable resources" would amount to over 200 billion bbl of oil and 32 tcm of natural gas in SSA only (International Energy Agency 2014). Such disparities indicate that there is a significant uncertainty surrounding the hydrocarbon endowment of Africa, and particularly in SSA where hydrocarbon basins have generally been explored to a lesser extent.

Figure 2.1 is a map of all Africa's sedimentary basins identified so far with acknowledged or presumed hydrocarbon potential (32 out of 60 are under explo-ration or awaiting exploration). It is immediately visible that most of the oil and gas is found in "continental margin basins" along the coastline. In fact, a large part of the oil available in SSA (70%), as well as much of the production, comes from deep or ultra-deep water offshore fields.

Basins names: 1, Andalusian-Pre-Rif; 2, Western Tell; 3, Southern Tell; 4, Eastern Tell; 5, Eastern Atlas; 6, Tunisia–Sicily; 7, Middle Atlas; 8, Central Atlas; 9, Alge-rian–Libyan; 10, Sahara–East Mediterranean; 11, Gulf of Suez depression of the Red Sea–Suez basin; 12, West Moroccan; 13, Aaiun; 14, Tindouf; 15, Reggane; 16, Murzuq; 17, Kufra; 18, Red Sea depression of the Red Sea–Suez basin; 19, Senegal; 20, Taoudeni; 21, Mali–Niger; 22, Chad; 23, Gao; 24, Leone–Liberian; 25, Volta; 26, Chari; 27, Upper Nile; 28, South Aden; 29, Gulf of Guinea; 30, East African; 31,

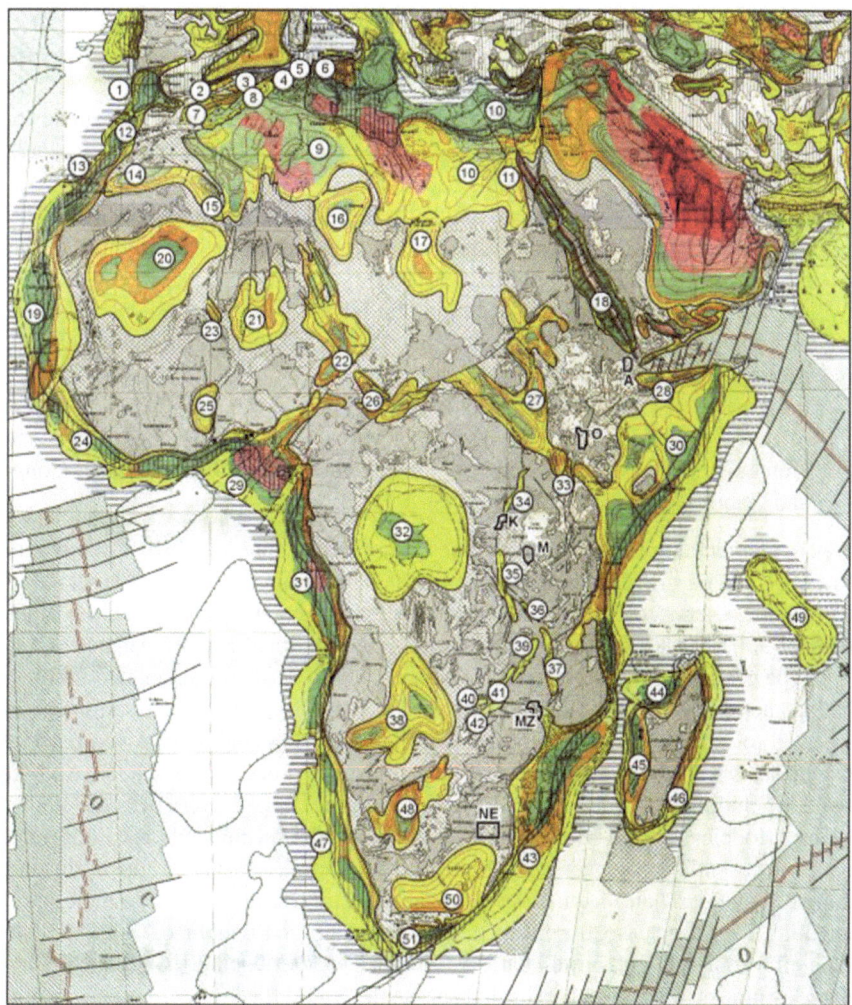

Fig. 2.1 Sedimentary basins with known or yet-to-find hydrocarbon potential. *Source* Modelevsky and Modelevsky (2016)

Kwanza–Cameroon; 32, Congo; 33, Turkana; 34, Albert; 35, Tanganyika; 36, Rukwa; 37, Nyasa; 38, Okavango; 39, Luangwa; 40, Kafue; 41, Luano; 42, Kariba; 43, Mozambique; 44, Majunga; 45, Morondava; 46, Eastern Madagascar; 47, Namibia; 48, Kalahari; 49, Seyshelles; 50, Karoo; 51, South Cape; A, Afar; K, Kivu; M, Malagarasi; O, Omo; MZ, Middle Zambezi; NE, basins of the northeastern part of South Africa.

Looking specifically at SSA, the following regions host major hydrocarbon basins at different levels of exploration and exploitation (International Energy Agency 2014)

I. the Niger Delta. This is the best known, most exploited, and richest hydrocarbon basin in the region. Reserves are located in the offshore territory of Nigeria, Cameroon, and Equatorial Guinea;

II. the East African Rift. Recent discoveries of oil have been made in Uganda and Kenya and exploration is ongoing in Democratic Republic of Congo, Rwanda, Burundi, Tanzania and Ethiopia;

III. the East African Coast. Major discoveries of gas have been made in the offshore territory of Mozambique and Tanzania, and geological surveys point at further resources in Seychelles and Madagascar;

IV. the West African Transform Margin. Initial discoveries of oil resources are awaiting the assessment of commercial viability in Ghana, Liberia, Mauritania, Sierra Leone, and Ivory Coast;

V. the West Coast Pre-Salt. Exploration is ongoing in the deep layers of basins offshore of Angola, Namibia, and all the way up to Congo, Gabon, Equatorial Guinea, and Cameroon. Recent major discoveries have been made in Congo and Gabon (James and Wright 2016).

A fundamental question when it comes to non-renewable sources is for how long extraction can be sustained before complete depletion. At current rates of extraction, recoverable reserves of African oil should last for around 100 years, and those of gas for over 900 years (assuming no gas flaring) (International Energy Agency 2014). This type of estimate (ratio of reserves on production, R/P) compares two numbers that can actually vary quite significantly in time. In SSA, rates of extraction can be expected to increase significantly following growing demand, but proven reserves may do so as well. Future discoveries could be expected in currently under-explored basins (including in Central Africa), as well as in the deeper layers of better known basins (Modelevsky and Modelevsky 2016). Also, the recent shale revolution that makes it possible to recover unconventional oil and gas that is "trapped" in fine-grained rock (i.e. shale) formations, is making many countries reassess their actual potential. This is the case, for instance, of the Democratic Republic of Congo with its shale oil resource of 100 billion barrels (World Energy Council 2016), South Africa, where estimates indicate 11 tcm of shale gas in the Karoo Basin (International Energy Agency 2014), and Algeria, which has one of the largest shale gas reserves in the world (20 tcm) (Tagliapietra 2017).

The biggest oil producers in SSA today are Nigeria and Angola, together accounting for almost half of the entire African production (Table 2.1). In North African countries, Algeria and Libya have similar production levels, although since the civil war of 2011 Libya has been producing far below its potential. Oil is also extracted in many other SSA countries. Some, like South Sudan and Chad, have quite high R/P ratio, indicating that there is a certain potential to increase production—at least in principle, because of course the profitability of investments depends on many factors, among which access to global markets, global oil prices (notoriously unpredictable) as well as country-specific political, financial, and security risks. All in all, oil investments in SSA tend to be less attractive than in other resource-rich regions,

Table 2.1 Oil reserves and production (2016)

Country	Proved oil reserves (billion bbl)	Reserves-to-production (R/P) ratio	Oil production (thousand bbl/day)
Algeria	12.2	21.1	1,579
Egypt	3.5	13.7	691
Libya	48.4	310.1	426
Tunisia	0.4	18.4	63
Angola	11.6	17.5	1,807
Chad	1.5	56.1	73
Congo	1.6	18.4	238
Equatorial Guinea	1.1	10.7	280
Gabon	2.0	24.1	227
Nigeria	37.1	49.3	2,053
South Sudan	3.5	80.9	118
Sudan	1.5	39.6	104
Others	3.7	43.2	233
Total Africa	128.0	44.3	7,892

Source British Petroleum (2017b)
Note According to ENI, other countries with proved reserves of over 0.1 billion barrels include: Cameroon, Ivory Coast, Democratic Republic of Congo, Ghana, and Tunisia (ENI 2017a)

and the reason is to be found precisely the presence of these risks (International Energy Agency 2014).

Notwithstanding difficulties, new oil markets are taking shape (e.g. Uganda and Kenya) and others are strengthening (e.g. Ghana, which in 2016–2017 has been boosting production to the point of doubling its oil revenues (Oxford Business Group 2017)). Notably, the growth of SSA oil production today is driven by small producers, though most of them may already start experiencing a decline in production as early as 2020. A similar future is expected for the oil giant Angola. In contrast, Nigeria, Kenya, Uganda, and even South Africa (if counting synthetic fuel produced via coal-to-liquid transformation) are expected to boost production (International Energy Agency 2014).

When it comes to natural gas, the situation is not too dissimilar (Table 2.2). About 90% of Africa's natural gas production comes from Algeria, Egypt, Libya, and Nigeria, which dominates SSA's production. Once again, there are important prospective newcomers, notably Mozambique and Tanzania that are currently evaluating the opportunities available to make use of their newly discovered reserves—their potential being estimated at 2.8 and 1.3 tcm, respectively (US Energy Information Administration 2014; Department for International Trade Tanzania, Government of the UK 2015). Other countries are also considering to scale up gas production, for instance Senegal (Reuters 2017).

Table 2.2 Gas reserves and production (2016)

Country	Proved gas reserves (tcm)	Reserves-to-production (R/P) ratio	Gas production (bcm)
Algeria	4.5	49.3	91.3
Egypt	1.8	44.1	41.8
Libya	1.5	149.2	10.1
Nigeria	5.3	117.7	44.9
Others	1.1	54.9	20.2
Total Africa	14.3	68.4	208.3

Source British Petroleum (2017b)
Note According to ENI, other countries with proved reserves of over 0.1 tcm include Angola, Cameroon, Congo, and Mozambique. These and others with lower reserves (e.g. Ivory Coast) have production in place (ENI 2017b)

About one sixth of proven natural gas reserves in SSA are associated with oil (International Energy Agency 2014), and gas flaring—the practice of burning associated gas from oil extraction—is widespread. On top of being a major waste of energy, this practice emits large amounts of CO_2. Nigeria is responsible of around 60% of SSA's gas flaring, and Angola, Congo, and Gabon follow. Fortunately, all of these countries are taking important steps towards solving the problem, either by starting to market the excess gas or by re-injecting it to sustain production.

2.1.2   Coal

Compared to oil and natural gas, proved coal reserves are much more geographically confined in the southern part of the continent (Fig. 2.2; Table 2.3). Of the total estimated 36 billion tonnes proven coal reserves in the subcontinent, 90% are located in South Africa. Coal reserves in Mozambique, Zimbabwe, and Botswana are also conspicuous (estimated 25 billion tonnes for the first two; 21 billion tonnes for the third), less so those of Malawi, Swaziland, Tanzania, and Zambia. Overall, a large part of SSA coal reserves are of high quality (anthracite and bituminous) (British Petroleum 2017b).

Considering the relative paucity of coal reserves in the continent (most of the global coal production takes place the northern hemisphere where the majority of coal reserves are located) the weight of South Africa really stands out: the country is the seventh largest producer in the world (British Petroleum 2017a). The coal industry in South Africa is also quite advanced, technologically speaking, and the country is a global leader in coal-to-liquids technology.

Apart from South Africa, which leads coal production in the region (95%), SSA coal reserves are largely undeveloped, the main reason being the remoteness of

Fig. 2.2 Coal deposits (red: anthracite and bituminous; green: lignite). *Source* (Britannica Online Encyclopaedia) 2010 © EB, Inc

Table 2.3 Coal reserves and production in Africa (2016)

Country 2016	Proved coal reserves (million tonnes)	Reserves-to-production (R/P) ratio	Coal production (million TOE)
South Africa	9,893	39	142.4
Zimbabwe	502	186	1.7
Others	2,822	276	6.3
Total Africa	13,217	–	150.4

Source British Petroleum (2017b)

potential mines and the lack of infrastructure (rails and ports) (International Energy Agency 2014). But there are also other reasons. In Nigeria for instance, despite a significant potential, there is relatively little production because the country historically prioritized developing oil (and more recently gas). In Tanzania, it was the poor quality of reserves that made the country reconsider investments in coal mining and coal based power production (Othieno and Awange 2016).

2.2   Demand

Oil demand is growing unequivocally across the subcontinent (it recently overtook coal as the most consumed source of energy in the region) and it is driven mainly by the transport sector. Oil is also important for power generation, including for back-up—a key feature of SSA industry. As anticipated, oil consumption in SSA remains very low if compared to the rest of the world and, of the entire regional demand, half of it comes from South Africa and Nigeria alone, which are also the only two countries with a noteworthy petrochemical industry (International Energy Agency 2014).

Natural gas is the least consumed of hydrocarbons in SSA today, but it is undoubtedly gaining importance. The most notable advantage of natural gas is that, when it comes to power production, it is a cheaper alternative to oil and a cleaner alternative to coal (and oil). However at the same time, the infrastructure required to handle it is the most complex because in order to be transported, natural gas needs to be either compressed (CNG) or liquefied (LNG) (Fig. 2.3). On top of being the largest producer, Nigeria is also by far the main consumer of natural gas in SSA, with 5.2 bcm consumed in 2015 followed from a distance by South Africa, with 2.3 bcm (Organization for Economic Co-operation and Development). The main sectors of gas consumption in Nigeria are power production (60%) and industrial uses such as cement and fertilizer production (Occhiali and Falchetta 2018), whereas in South Africa natural gas is used exclusively for the production of synthetic liquid fuels (Department of Energy, Republic of South Africa).

Figure 2.3 is a schematic representation of oil refining and gas processing, aimed at transforming raw materials into final petroleum products. These have very different properties that make them more or less suitable for different uses, however their actual demand is linked to availability as much as it is to the presence of subsidies. In fact particularly in developing countries, consumer subsidies for petroleum products are typically set up in order to facilitate access among the poorest—although quite often they end up benefiting the wealthier and creating market distortions (Whitley and van der Burg 2015).

North African countries rely on fossil fuels all across the spectrum of their economy (including agriculture and households) and they are heavily subsidised. Elsewhere in Africa too, prices of oil products are either subsidised (in producing countries) or at least regulated to protect consumers from global oil price fluctuations (International Energy Agency 2014). In general, in SSA the use of diesel is more widespread than gasoline both in the transport sector and for (back-up) power generation. For household consumption, on the other hand, kerosene and LPG are the most common substitutes to solid biomass. The first is a product of oil refining, while the second can be produced both from crude oil and natural gas processing. The use of these fuels is subsidized in most oil producing countries (especially kerosene) as well as in some importing countries with dedicated policies, like Senegal (LPG) (International Energy Agency 2014).

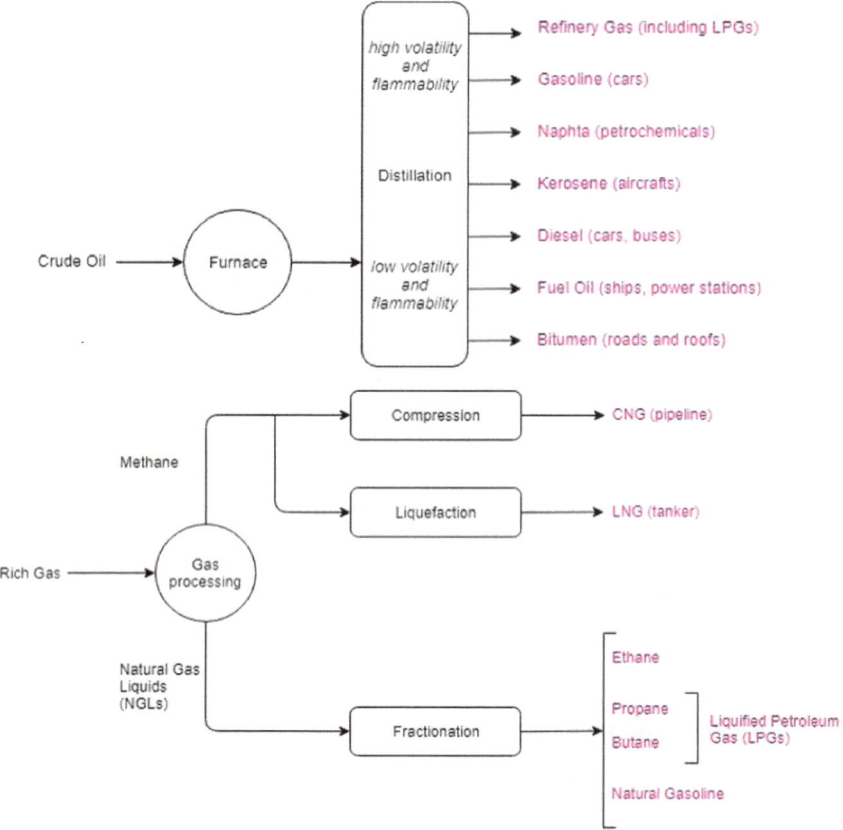

Fig. 2.3 Petroleum products from oil refining (above) and natural gas processing (below). *Sources* Author's elaboration. *Note* Petrol is synonym of gasoline; Paraffin is kerosene; Pipeline NG is CNG

The demand of coal is strictly linked to power production, with the exception of South Africa where coal is also processed for other uses. Because of its vast reserves, the country built up its entire energy system around coal, which supplies 70% of the total primary demand of the country mostly in the form of electricity, but also as synthetic diesel for the transport sector (covering about 40% of demand) and coal gas (i.e. the product of gasification of coal) used in industry and the residential sector (Department of Energy, Republic of South Africa). In SSA, coal-to-power takes place in small electricity-producing countries that sometime rely heavily on it, like Botswana (96% of total power production), Mauritius (42%), Niger (71%) and Zimbabwe (44%). While many more plan to increase coal-fired power production or introduce it (e.g. Malawi) and the sector can attract international investors (see Chap. 5), a relatively low number of power plants are actually under construction in SSA (End Coal).

2.3 Energy Trade (Out of Africa)

While demand of hydrocarbons is growing, Africa is still the energy macro-region with the lowest average oil and gas consumption in the world, and in terms of coal consumption is only second to the coal-poor regions of Middle East and South America (British Petroleum 2017b). This is because, with a few exceptions, domestic markets are poorly developed, and the bulk of hydrocarbon resources extracted in SSA is devoted to exports. Oil and gas investments in SSA feed the upstream oil and gas sector (extraction) much more than the midstream (refining and transport) and downstream (distribution) industry.

Most oil producing countries, including Angola and Nigeria, export over 85% of their production to Europe, Asia, and the US. The same is true for gas from Nigeria, Equatorial Guinea, and Mozambique, and prospects for exports are particularly bright now that with offshore gas liquefaction facilities (FLNG) it is possible to step in global LNG markets without developing potentially unsecure onshore infrastructure (Reuters 2017). Even coal trade leans towards inter-continental export, not only from South Africa but also from smaller producers, like Mozambique and Nigeria (International Energy Agency 2014).

A remarkable fact is that, when it comes to oil and gas products like LPG, gasoline, diesel, and so on, SSA relies almost entirely on imports from Europe and the Middle East (Fig. 2.4). Both the weight of crude oil export, as well as the importance of imports vis-à-vis final demand, are immediately clear glancing at Fig. 2.5, which is a representation of the oil production sector in Nigeria in 2013.

Exporting fossil fuels (like other mining products) is a major source of income for African countries, however governments typically fail to effectively reinvest fiscal revenues in the development of internal energy markets.

2.4 Insufficient Infrastructure

As anticipated in Chap. 2, the lack of infrastructure necessary to process, transport and distribute energy to the final users is a characteristic of the SSA region in contrast with South Africa, with its fairly decent power grid, and the North African region with its far-reaching power and gas infrastructure.

The fact that oil production is oriented to exports (5 million barrels per day), while the region is dependent on oil products import (1 million barrel per day), highlights the inadequacy of refineries, which are few and poorly maintained. This way, SSA countries miss out on the opportunity to export high-margin refined products (e.g. gasoline) and tend to import lower quality ones like heavy diesel (that western countries find difficult to sell at home due to environmental regulation).

The only country in the subcontinent with a major capacity of refineries is South Africa, which serves about two thirds of its own domestic demand of oil products. Some small producing countries (like Cameroon, Chad, Ivory Coast, Niger) are self-

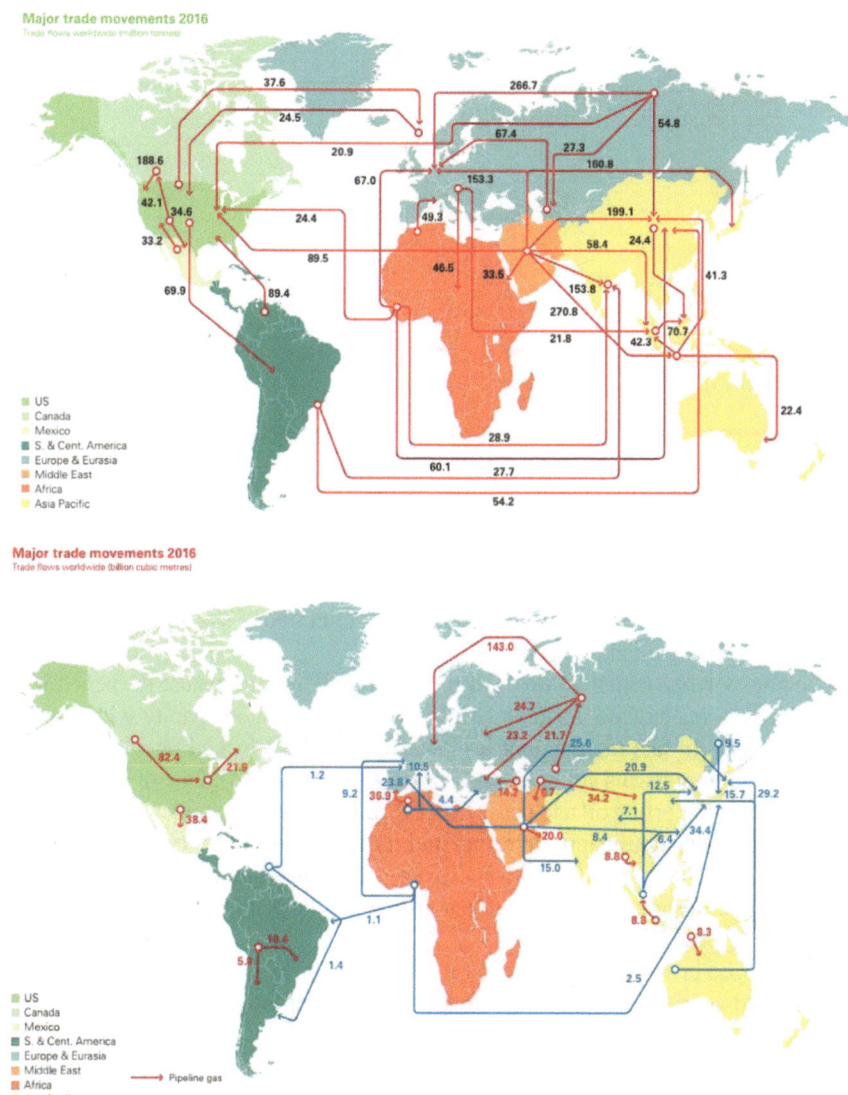

Fig. 2.4 Global trade of oil (above) and gas (below) (2016). *Source* British Petroleum (2017b). *Note* inter-regional flows reported in the map do not correspond to actual import/export routes

sufficient with their own refineries, but this is in stark contrast with the rest of SSA. On top of having low refining capacities, the utilization rates of refineries are low and declining: the average in Africa today is 60% in 2016, the lowest of all continents (British Petroleum 2017b). In fact, there are both financial and logistical constraints

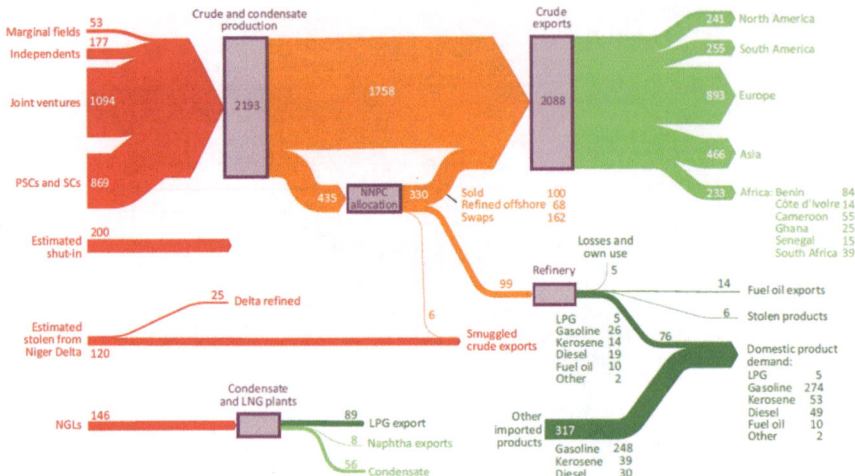

Fig. 2.5 Nigerian oil production sector. *Source* International Energy Agency (2014)

related to building new capacity and securing a continuous supply of crude oil to existing processing plants.

The transport and distribution of fossil fuels is challenging because the penetration of pipelines is inadequate—and so is, generally, the storage capacity within countries (Fig. 2.6). In fact many countries—particularly land-locked ones—are highly vulnerable to import cuts (International Energy Agency 2014). One of the practical problems of transporting oil and gas is the occurrence of theft episodes along pipeline tracks, which can significantly interrupt and reduce supply flows (see the weight of oil theft in Nigeria in Fig. 2.4). Moreover, it is not uncommon that pipelines need to cross dangerous areas where insurgent groups can tactically damage them or take control of supply.

Plans, more or less advanced, exist to build pipelines or other connections (via rail and road as in the case of South Sudan-Djibouti-Ethiopia) in:

- Kenya (Omondi 2018): oil;
- Uganda-Tanzania (Business Daily 2016): oil;
- South Sudan-Djibouti-Ethiopia (The Reporter Ethiopia 2017) (Ford 2017): oil;
- Mozambique-South Africa (Macauhub 2011) (Business Report 2017): oil and gas;
- Mozambique-Botswana (Zimbabwe Independent 2018) (extension of Mozambique-Zimbabwe) oil;
- From Nigeria to Algeria (trans-Saharan (Business Day 2017): gas;
- From Nigeria-Morocco, offshore (The North African Post 2017): gas.

When it comes to natural gas, the high cost of mid- and downstream (i.e. transport and distribution) infrastructure has been one of the main hindrances to the development of domestic gas industries in SSA countries. The gas pipeline in Nigeria that takes natural gas from the Niger delta to the interiors of the country is so far the only

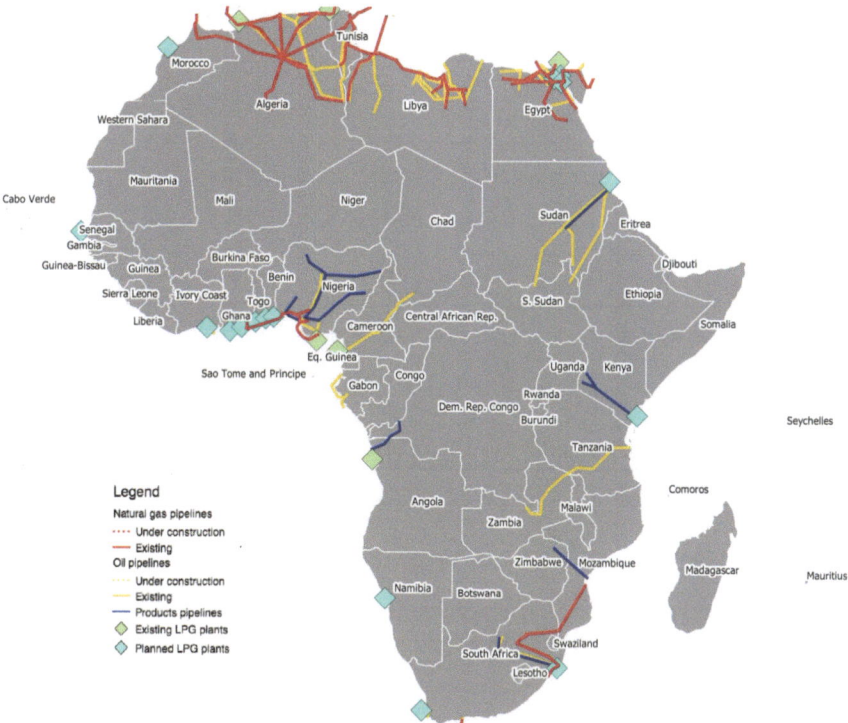

Fig. 2.6 Oil and gas infrastructure. *Source* authors' elaboration. Information from (Theodora) (International Energy Agency 2014; Corbeau 2016)

example in SSA of a gas network built for internal distribution, and its management is far from smooth. This pipeline has been constantly affected by intermittency of supply due to the occurrence of theft and vandalism episodes, which delayed significantly its construction and casted doubts on the profitability of its potential extension. Exporting gas ends up being a safer choice for international companies: indeed, they regularly prioritise export over domestic supply despite having legal obligations to serve domestic demands first (Occhiali and Falchetta 2018).

2.5 A Long-Term Perspective on Fossil Fuel Development

Fossil fuels can help energizing SSA, but their development is not going to be straightforward. Particularly in the power sector, renewables are starting to compete with fossil fuels—even on costs, and even in Africa (Fig. 2.7). The dilemma of SSA governments is clear: should they take the risk of building infrastructural, carbon lock-ins around fossil fuels? The question is perhaps even broader than this: should they even

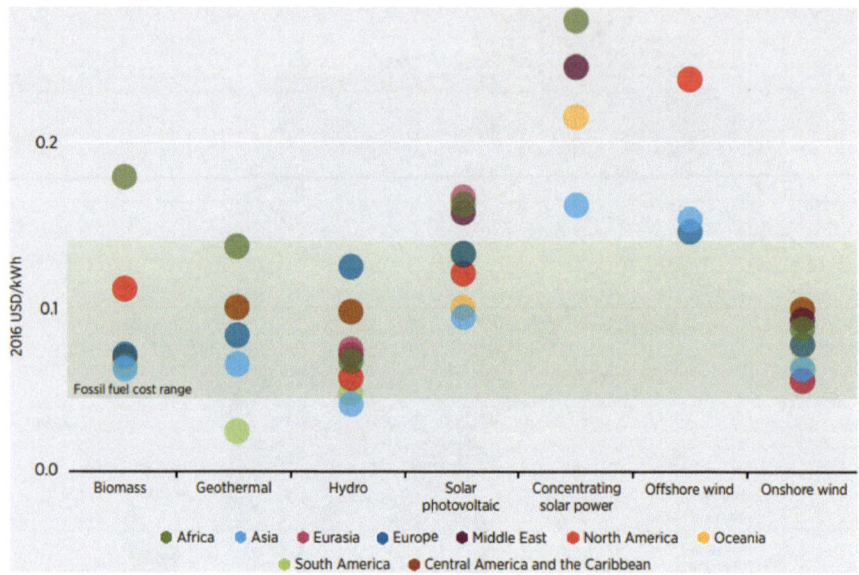

Fig. 2.7   Regional weighted average levelised cost of electricity by technology. *Source* International Renewable Energy Agency (2018) © IRENA 2018

aim at embarking on a path dependency on energy-intensive development (Fouquet 2016)? At the end of the day, it will be up to each single country to envision its own energy policy and, if available, how to value hydrocarbon reserves. It is therefore worth taking a fresh look at the benefits that fossil fuels can deliver in SSA as well as the issues that they will carry with them in the long run.

One first consideration goes to the opportunity of "leapfrogging" coal: the timing is good. Global projections paint a bleak picture for the sector, which is experiencing record rates of decline in production and consumption and receives less and less support from international financing institutions (British Petroleum 2017b; International Energy Agency 2017a) (Shankleman and Warren 2017). South Africa—the coal giant—is also under pressure to diversify its energy mix now that the most accessible mines are depleting and new mines will require significant investments (International Energy Agency 2014). Still, coal is far from dead in Africa. Even in Morocco, where renewable energy plays such a big role in the country's vision of a sustainable development, coal remains an integral part of the power system.

Climate and environmental concerns are resonating in the international community, so much so that international financial institutions now tend to support almost exclusively renewable energy projects because they do not come with the trade-off of climate emissions. And while coal is the most under pressure, it is not alone. Emblematically, the World Bank Group recently announced it will no longer support upstream oil and gas projects, starting from 2019 (World Bank 2017). This will not, of course, put a halt to investments, but the difference is that country institutions willing to attract private investors in oil, gas, and coal will have to negotiate directly with them.

While the interest of international investors in African oil and gas is high, doing business in Africa is not easy. Overall, the main challenges that oil and gas investors face in Africa are related to political instability and the lack of clear fiscal regimes and legal frameworks, generalized corruption, poor infrastructural base, and lack of skilled resources (PwC 2017). Fortunately, many countries are putting more pressure on oil and gas developers to ensure certain levels of production to supply internal markets first, to improve local content, or to respect environmental standards, but without a parallel commitment to making energy governance more efficient and transparent, this may only result in investors losing interest (Ernst & Young 2014).

In SSA the weight of renewable energy in the electrification process will be unprecedented, bringing not only solutions to remote areas off-grid, but also opening opportunities for large scale, clean and cheap power generation (Chap. 4). While in principle renewables and fossil fuels are not mutually exclusive, their competition may lead to sub-optimal consequences. Notably, without dedicated policies, cheap renewables may end up displacing natural gas instead of the more polluting, and much less versatile coal even where the first one is domestically available (de Strasser et al. 2017). Similarly, without a concrete vision to eradicate the use of solid biomass using all sensible means, the potential role of natural gas and LPG as cooking fuels risks being underplayed in favour of other, less effective solutions.

2.5.1 Natural Gas Potential

Natural gas has a strategic advantage over other fossil fuels in the sector of power generation. Like coal, natural gas can provide a steady supply to urban and industrial areas but crucially, gas fired plants are also a better fit to variable renewable energies, thanks to their higher operational flexibility and lower capital cost. With the deployment of the huge renewable energy potential in Africa, most of which is variable and not dispatchable (like solar and wind), there will be a need for dispatchable power plants which will operate in mid-load: it is here that gas has an advantage over coal (Gonzalez-Salazar et al. 2018). Gas fired power generation is often cheaper than coal based power generation, in fact the investment cost of a gas fired power plant are half (combined cycle) or a quarter (gas turbine) compared to a coal fired power plant. Operating costs are higher if gas prices are high, but they may be quite low if gas is domestic and cannot be exported easily.

Notably, natural gas is the cleanest among fossil fuels. While greenhouse gas emissions from the industry are not negligible, the potential to abate them is quite high and reasonably cheap to realize. However, the real environmental advantage of using gas is the cleanliness on the user side: less air pollution, reduced risk of land and water contamination.

Most of the environmental impact of natural gas occurs upstream, which is where responsible planning will be critical to avoid ecological damage. A serious issue to be considered carefully is the viability of shale gas fracking, particularly in water-scarce regions where the risk of groundwater contamination is perhaps not worth taking.

International pipelines for natural gas require high investments. And, more critically, they are considered fixed links, whereby a geopolitical conflict may result in pipelines to become idle (there many examples of this phenomenon in the Middle East). LNG chains, though also being very capital intensive, are much more flexible, as tankers can easily change destination en route, if needed. This flexibility should motivate global LNG producers—as well as current and perspective African ones—to sell in Africa and even pioneering the creation of new markets there. Potential African producers include Mozambique and Tanzania, who would add to the already established production in the west coast (Angola, Nigeria and Equatorial Guinea). Other than Egypt who is already a LNG buyer (temporarily: until its own production builds up again), today's potential LNG importers include Benin, Ivory Coast, Ghana, Kenya, Morocco, Namibia, Senegal, South Africa, and Sudan. Clearly, importing LNG is mainly an opportunity for coastal countries, but can also be seen as the beginning of further cross-country trade (Corbeau 2016).

In practice, the presence of large power plants or big industrial players like steel, cement, or even fertilizer production to which natural gas is a feedstock, is a necessary condition for residential uses to kick-off (even though not sufficient). In SSA, a promising model to develop internal gas markets seems to be starting from gas-to-power (i.e. using power producers as anchor customers) supported by floating regasification units (FSRU—Floating Storage Regasification Unit). These are faster to build and easier to operate than traditional regasification units, and when demand of LNG imports is no longer there (for instance because own gas production has taken off) the FSRU can just be moved to another country. There are already many examples worldwide of this new technology. Today in Africa only Egypt uses one, but projects at different stages of development exist in Ghana, Morocco, South Africa, Namibia and Kenya. Once "anchored" to power production, the availability of gas may stimulate the demand of industry, transport, and cooking.

For the latter a caveat is needed. In general, it does not make economic sense to build a gas distribution system exclusively for cooking. Notably, if there is no demand for residential heating—as it would be the case in Africa—the relatively modest volumes of natural gas demanded for cooking does not justify the investment in distribution infrastructure. Furthermore, the horizontal and often informal expansion of most urban agglomerates in Africa makes distribution costly, and risky. That said, natural gas distribution could target high-income, densely populated neighbourhoods in cities where gas is available, like Accra (Ghana), Lagos (Nigeria), or Abidjan (Ivory Coast) but it is clear that this type of investment would require considerable motivation and explicit support from the side of policy makers.

2.5.2 The Case of LPG for Cooking

Today, LPG (i.e. propane, butane, or a mix of the two) is already the most utilised alternative to solid biomass for cooking in SSA; still, only 7% of SSA's population have access to it and LPG use is mostly concentrated in a few countries: Angola, Ghana, Nigeria, and Sudan (International Energy Agency 2017b). LPG can be used for multiple purposes, including transport, but in SSA its real potential probably lies in its use as a modern cooking fuel—as well as, once available, as heat for small income generating activities like food processing, brick making, metal casting, and so on (McDade 2004).

Together with ethanol, methanol, biogas, and electricity, LPG is among the few cooking fuels that can meet the indoor pollution standards set by the World Health Organization, and several studies point at its suitability for cooking in the developing world. In particular, when compared to kerosene which is the second most utilised fossil-fuel based cooking fuel, LPG is much less hazardous to handle.

However the case for LPG can—and should—be made even without claiming that it is the best available option. As explained in Chap. 1, the lack of clean cooking in SSA is a social plague that can be truly addressed only with the parallel promotion of a mix of all available alternatives. LPG is a valuable option, but its wide uptake requires a significant policy effort. In fact, consumers (both urban and rural) base their choices not only on the availability of alternatives, but also on opportunity costs, and cooking preferences.

The truth is, subsidies play a major role in determining which fuel is preferred by users. The experience of Senegal is emblematic: after a successful strategy, LPG ended up reaching as much as 70% of urban users, but as soon as the government decided to lift subsidies there was a massive drop in consumption. Hence, if the ambition is to bring LPG cooking also to rural users, the most critical elements of success will be the existence of far reaching LPG value chains on the one hand and the effectiveness of targeted pro-poor cross-subsidization on the other. It is not excluded that smarter payment methods could also help accelerating access to LPG distribution (the same way this is happening with solar lanterns—see Chap. 4), either as a purely market-driven solution or in combination with subsidies. So far, however, the accumulated experience in implementing this solution is still limited (International Energy Agency 2017b).

Particularly for rural customers, accessibility remains highly problematic. The distribution of LPG from production sites or import stations to the single users requires the careful handling, storage, and transport, of pressurised gas (in comparison, the transport of liquid kerosene is less complicated). Clearly, this type of supply chain cannot be improvised for safety reasons, and a multitude of factors like the poor state of roads in rural SSA or the handling of pressurized cylinders by untrained people, can become significant elements of risk.

Despite these issues, there is ample evidence that—once available and affordable—LPG responds to the needs of customers, which is not trivial. For instance, the experience of South Africa shows that (subsidised) LPG cooking can take root even where electrical cooking is available and cheap (Kimemia and Annegarn 2016). At the same time in India—where the use of solid biomass is also widespread—LPG seems to be responsible of the first signs of reduction in solid biomass consumption after decades of promotion of improved biomass stoves, which ended up delivering poor results (International Energy Agency 2017b).

LPG is not a new solution, and its promotion in different parts of the world has already resulted in both success stories and failures. Some SSA countries like Ghana, Cameroon, and Senegal are already embarking in ambitious LPG programs, but experience is also accumulating on larger scales in countries like China, Brazil, India, and Indonesia as well as in North Africa, where LPG is commonly used.

In sum, promoting LPG requires a high level of economic, infrastructural, and logistic commitment, but it is also a fairly effective solution not to be missed for resolving the pressing problem of unsafe cooking. Notably, women are the best positioned promoters of clean cooking solutions because they are the first beneficiaries of improved indoor pollution and reduced time for cooking, which is why linking LPG programs to gender-focused and women-led development initiatives could prove crucial (Energy Sector Management Assistance Program, World Bank 2014).

2.5.3 Managing Air Pollution from the Energy Sector

As plans for coal become concrete, the main concern of SSA policy makers should not be so much on greenhouse gases—which they arguably have the right to emit, and which impact would nevertheless be lower than that of western countries—but on particulates. According to a recent estimate, air pollution from coal fired generation causes 2,200 deaths annually in South Africa and costs the government 2.37 billion dollars per year (Holland 2017).

Another important contributor to air pollution is transport. The sector is driving the demand of oil in SSA, however as of today environmental regulation on vehicles is basically inexistent in most countries. Only Nigeria and South Africa adopted Euro 2 emissions standards, and a limit on the age of imported vehicles has been imposed in a handful of countries only (International Energy Agency 2014). More could be done, also thinking in terms of urban planning. The direction is already set by several African NDCs[3] that mention plans to scale up mass transportation (e.g. buses, trains), the acquisition of hybrid vehicles for public transport, and the potential use of bio-fuels (Chap. 4) (UN Economic Commission for Africa 2016).

To be clear, the issue of air pollution goes beyond coal power production and oil-based transport. Although very difficult to quantify given the lack of emission inventories, estimates of deaths by air pollution indicate that the threat comes from a variety of sources. In contrast to western countries where air pollution comes largely

---

[3]National Determined Contributions to reduce greenhouse gas emissions and adapt to the impact of climate change, submitted to UN Framework Convention on Climate Change (UNFCCC) by the signatories of the Paris Agreement on Climate (2015).

(circa 50%) from vehicle emissions, in SSA solid biomass and waste burning are probably the biggest factors (the latter being particularly hard to quantify because of the unknown chemical composition of emissions from composite waste).

Since 1990, while the number of premature deaths related to unsafe water, lack of sanitation facilities, and malnutrition have been declining in SSA, those related to indoor and ambient air pollution have increased (Roy 2016). This highlights the importance of tackling the problem from multiple sides, including the capillary, uncontrolled use of solid biomass.

References

Bailis R, Drigo R, Ghilardi A, Masera O (2015) The carbon footprint of traditional woodfuels. Nat Clim Change. Vol 5 Nr 3

Britannica Online Encyclopaedia Coal deposits. https://www.britannica.com/media/full/122863/1 42296. Accessed 10 Apr 2018

British Petroleum (2017a) BP Statistical Review 2017—Africa's energy market in 2016

British Petroleum (2017b) Statistical review of world energy 2017

Business Daily (2016) What Uganda-Tanzania crude oil pipeline pact means for Kenya. In: Bus. Dly. https://www.businessdailyafrica.com/analysis/What-Uganda-Tanzania-crude-oil-pipe line-pact-means-for-Kenya/539548-3108134-1301mm7z/index.html. Accessed 7 Mar 2018

Business Day (2017) ICRC partners NEPAD on Trans-Saharan gas pipeline project. In: BusinessDay news you can trust. http://www.businessdayonline.com/icrc-partners-nepad-trans-saharan-gas-p ipeline-project/. Accessed 7 Mar 2018

Business Report (2017) New SA and Mozambique gas pipelines to meet demand| IOL Business Report. https://www.iol.co.za/business-report/new-sa-and-mozambique-gas-pipelines-to-meet-d emand-11535938. Accessed 7 Mar 2018

Corbeau A-S (2016) LNG for Africa, King Abdullah Petroleum Studies and Research Center (KAPSARC)

de Strasser L, Tagliapietra S, Hafner M (2017) Renewables and gas: what mix to solve Sub-Saharan Africa's energy access challenge? FEEM Brief

Department for International Trade Tanzania, Government of the UK (2015) Oil and gas export opportunities in Tanzania for UK companies. https://www.gov.uk/government/news/oil-and-ga s-export-opportunities-in-tanzania-for-uk-companies. Accessed 22 Feb 2018

Department of Energy, Republic of South Africa Natural gas overview. http://www.energy.gov.za/ files/naturalgas_frame.html. Accessed 27 Feb 2018

End Coal Global Coal Plant Tracker. In: End coal. https://endcoal.org/tracker/. Accessed 12 Apr 2017

Energy Sector Management Assistance Program, World Bank (2014) Cooking with gas: why women in developing countries want LPG and how they can get it

ENI (2017a) World oil review 2017

ENI (2017b) World gas and renewables review 2017

Ernst & Young (2014) 10 hotspots in African oil & gas. In: Offshore energy today. https://www.of fshoreenergytoday.com/10-hotspots-in-african-oil-gas-infographic/. Accessed 28 Feb 2018

Ford N (2017) South Sudan-Ethiopia road opens up trade route. Afr Bus Mag

Fouquet R (2016) Path dependence in energy systems and economic development. Nat Energy 1:16098. https://doi.org/10.1038/nenergy.2016.98

Gonzalez-Salazar MA, Kirsten T, Prchlik L (2018) Review of the operational flexibility and emissions of gas- and coal-fired power plants in a future with growing renewables. Renew Sustain Energy Rev 82:1497–1513. https://doi.org/10.1016/j.rser.2017.05.278

Holland M (2017) Health impacts of coal fired power plants in South Africa. Cent Environ Rights. https://cer.org.za/news/air-pollution-from-coal-power-stations-causes-disease-and-kills-thousands-of-south-africans-every-year-says-uk-expert. Accessed 28 Feb 2018

International Energy Agency (2014) Africa energy outlook—a focus on energy prospects in Sub-Saharan Africa (World Energy Outlook Special Report)

International Energy Agency (2017a) World energy outlook

International Energy Agency (2017b) Energy access outlook (World Energy Outlook Special Report)

International Renewable Energy Agency (2018) Renewable power generation costs in 2017

James W, Wright S (2016) Pre-salt of West Africa, twin or distant relative of Brazil sub-surface? In: Gaffney Clien Assoc. http://gaffney-cline-focus.com/. Accessed 21 Feb 2018

Kimemia D, Annegarn H (2016) Domestic LPG interventions in South Africa: challenges and lessons. Energy Policy 93:150–156. https://doi.org/10.1016/j.enpol.2016.03.005

Krikorian S, Evrensel A (2017) Global nuclear power capacity through 2050. Int At Energy Agency. https://www.iaea.org/newscenter/news/iaea-releases-projections-on-global-nuclear-power-capacity-through-2050. Accessed 28 Feb 2018

Macauhub (2011) Petroline postpones construction of oil pipeline linking Mozambique to South Africa. In: Macauhub. https://macauhub.com.mo/2011/08/18/petroline-postpones-construction-of-oil-pipeline-linking-mozambique-to-south-africa/. Accessed 7 Mar 2018

McDade S (2004) Fueling development: the role of LPG in poverty reduction and growth. Energy Sustain Dev 8:74–81. https://doi.org/10.1016/S0973-0826(08)60469-X

Modelevsky MS, Modelevsky MM (2016) Assessment of the discovered and undiscovered oil and gas of Africa. Russ Geol Geophys 57:1342–1348. https://doi.org/10.1016/j.rgg.2016.08.019

Occhiali G, Falchetta G (2018) The changing role of natural gas in Nigeria. A policy outlook for energy security and sustainable development. FEEM Working Paper

Omondi G (2018) Total to built Kenya's crude pipeline to Lamu. In: East Africa http://www.theeastafrican.co.ke/business/Total-build-Kenya-Turkana-Lamu-crude-oil-pipeline/2560-4275772-2lflfsz/index.html. Accessed 7 Mar 2018

Organization for Economic Co-operation and Development OECD data. http://data.oecd.org. Accessed 10 Jan 2018

Othieno H, Awange J (2016) Energy resources in Africa. distribution, opportunities and challenges. Springer, Berlin

Oxford Business Group (2017) Ghana doubles energy revenue with increased oil production. In: OilPrice. https://oilprice.com/Energy/Crude-Oil/Ghana-Doubles-Energy-Revenue-With-Increased-Oil-Production.html. Accessed 21 Feb 2018

PwC (2017) Africa's oil & gas sector continues to show growth. In: PwC South Africa. https://www.pwc.co.za/en/press-room/oil-gas-africa-continent.html. Accessed 1 Mar 2018

Reuters (2017) African LNG exports to get boost from offshore projects. In: Reuters. https://www.reuters.com/article/africa-lng/african-lng-exports-to-get-boost-from-offshore-projects-idUSL5N1KI5W9

Roy R (2016) The cost of air pollution in Africa. OECD Development Centre Working Paper 333

Sathaye J, Lucon O, Rahman A, Christensen J, Denton F, Fujino J, Heath G, Kadner S, Mirza M, Rudnick H, Schlaepfer A, Shmakin A (2011) Renewable energy in the context of sustainable development. In: IPCC special report on renewable energy sources and climate change mitigation. Cambridge University Press

Shankleman J, Warren H (2017) Solar power will kill coal faster than you think. In: Bloomberg.com. https://www.bloomberg.com/news/articles/2017-06-15/solar-power-will-kill-coal-sooner-than-you-think. Accessed 21 Jun 2017

Tagliapietra S (2017) Energy relations in the Euro-Mediterranean. Palgrave Macmillan

The North African Post (2017) Moroccan-Nigerian pipeline puts final nail in Algeria's Trans-Saharan gas project. North Afr Post. http://northafricapost.com/17999-moroccan-nigerian-pipeline-puts-final-nail-algerias-trans-saharan-gas-project.html. Accessed 7 Mar 2018

The Reporter Ethiopia (2017) Gov. cancels planned Ethio-Djibouti oil pipeline project. https://www.thereporterethiopia.com/article/gov-cancels-planned-ethio-djibouti-oil-pipeline-project. Accessed 7 Mar 2018

Theodora Africa Pipelines Map. Theodora—Ctries World. https://theodora.com/pipelines/africa_oil_gas_and_products_pipelines_map.html. Accessed 7 Mar 2018

UN Economic Commission for Africa (2016) Transforming Africa's transport sector with the implementation of intended nationally determined contributions

US Energy Information Administration (2014) Monthly generator capacity factor data now available by fuel and technology—today in energy—U.S. Energy Information Administration (EIA). https://www.eia.gov/todayinenergy/detail.php?id=14611. Accessed 9 Jan 2018

Whitley S, van der Burg L (2015) Fossil fuel subsidy reform in sub-Saharan Africa: from rhetoric to reality. New Climate Economy, London and Washington, DC

World Bank (2017) Announcements at one planet summit. In: World Bank. http://www.worldbank.org/en/news/press-release/2017/12/12/world-bank-group-announcements-at-one-planet-summit. Accessed 28 Feb 2018

World Energy Council (2016) World energy resources. Oil

World Nuclear Association (2017) Uranium in Africa. World Nucl Assoc. http://www.world-nuclear.org/information-library/country-profiles/others/uranium-in-africa.aspx. Accessed 28 Feb 2018

Zimbabwe Independent (2018) Zim revives fuel pipeline deal with Bots. Zimb Indep. https://www.theindependent.co.zw/2018/02/23/zim-revives-fuel-pipeline-deal-bots/. Accessed 7 Mar 2018

Chapter 3
Prospects for Renewable Energy in Africa

Abstract Not long ago renewable power generation was an expensive choice to be subsidised by industrialized governments to signal an intention to shift to clean energy, however today renewable resources are becoming strategic assets for developing countries too, as the global industry grows stronger and the cost of technology falls dramatically. Their potential is particularly evident in Africa where solar, wind, hydro, geothermal, and biomass resources are abundant. While it is becoming evident that renewables have a major role to play in the electrification process of many countries in the region—including at small scale and off-grid—several challenges remain when it comes to establishing appropriate regulations, attracting foreign investments, and even sometimes simply setting clear targets. After describing the distribution of resources, this chapter looks at the policy frameworks in place in order to point at possible ways forward.

African countries are gifted with a huge—and still untapped—renewable energy potential. Estimates of power generation potential in the continent are 350 GW for hydroelectric, 110 GW for wind, 15 GW for geothermal and a staggering 1000 GW for solar (African Development Bank 2017). Potential for bioenergy is also high, with wood supply from surplus forest estimated at 520 GWh/year (International Renewable Energy Agency 2015). Solar is particularly promising in terms of geographical distribution: albeit with varying potentials, this type of energy could be harnessed virtually everywhere in Africa.

This large endowment of renewables is strategic for the continent, and the prospect of large-scale renewable power production may be a real game changer for several countries. While hydropower has been an option for a long time, other renewable solutions became commercially viable quite recently. Wind and solar in particular are now leading large-scale renewable power production across the continent, competing with fossil fuel alternatives also in terms of costs (Chap. 2).

In general, while many renewable energy sources can be used to produce electricity and/or heat without any combustion process (e.g. sunlight, wind, hydro, underground heat), others need to be burnt in order to release their energy (bioenergy from organic material, or biomass). While biomass is highly versatile—uses include

M. Hafner et al., *Energy in Africa*, SpringerBriefs in Energy,
https://doi.org/10.1007/978-3-319-92219-5_3

Table 3.1 Renewable energy in Africa

Modern renewable energy	Use
Firewood (improved cookstove)	Heat
Charcoal (improved cookstove)	
Ethanol (improved cookstove)	
Residue (industry)	
Briquettes (improved cookstove)	
Solar thermal (buildings and industry)	
Geothermal	Power
Solar PV	
Solar CSP (thermal)	
Wind	
Hydro	
Biomass (thermal)	
Biofuels	Transport

Source Elaborated from (International Renewable Energy Agency 2015)

cooking and heating, transport and electricity—it can be processed and utilized to different degrees of efficiency, cleanliness, and sustainability of the value chain. Unfortunately however, today's reliance on bioenergy in the primary energy mix of SSA (Chap. 2) only reflects the prevalence of rudimentary stoves for cooking with wood and charcoal (see Sect. 4.5).

Talking about *modern* renewable energy means considering ways of producing and consuming renewable energy that are as clean (in terms of particulate and carbon emissions) and as efficient as possible with today's technology (Table 3.1). Hence, modern renewables should replace or step up *traditional* uses of renewables in Africa, first and foremost the direct use of solid biomass.

When it comes to electricity production from renewables, a critical issue is that some of the best solutions (notably wind and solar) depend on a fluctuating source, hence their contribution to power generation is variable and sometimes even unpredictable. This is in contrast with fossil fuels and other renewables that are *dispatchable*, meaning that production can be regulated, initiated and ceased on demand, sometimes as quickly as within minutes, other times within hours. Geothermal, hydropower (reservoir type), concentrated solar power (CSP) enhanced with thermal storage, and biomass generation stand out as dispatchable renewables characterised by different degrees of output flexibility.

It should be noted that hydropower and biomass, unlike other renewables, rely on two critical natural resources—freshwater and biomass—that are increasingly demanded in SSA for multiple, sometimes conflicting uses, and that are subject to climate change impact through reduced rainfalls, higher temperatures, and desertification. Adapting to this reality will mean innovating and optimizing production

Table 3.2 Targets for renewables in selected countries

	Share of renewables in total power generation (%)	Solar (MW)	Wind (MW)	Hydro (MW)	Biomass (MW)	Geothermal (MW)
Angola			100	38	500	
Ghana	10%					
Kenya			636	1,320	44	2,300
Morocco		2,000	2,000	2,280	200	
Nigeria		6,831	292	8,174	3,211	
Rwanda		563	18.5		73	
Senegal	20%					
South Africa		9,600	9,200	75	12.5	
Sudan		716	680	56	54	2,228
Tanzania			100	3,541	100	
Tunisia		1,960	1,755		100	
Uganda				1,285	90	45
Zambia		150		100		

Source RISE website, accessed January 2018

processes, and finding smart synergies (e.g. valorising waste) so as to increase the overall efficiency of natural resource use (de Strasser 2017).

Some African countries are embarking in highly ambitious renewable power projects. Examples that aim at the top of global rankings of installed renewable capacity are: the Noor concentrated solar power plant in Morocco, Lake Turkana wind farm in Kenya, and the Grand Renaissance Dam in Ethiopia (total planned capacities of 500, 310 MW, and 6.45 GW respectively). Although the renewable energy sector is far from mature in most of SSA, today more and more countries are setting up targets for renewables (Table 3.2).

The fact that variable renewables will play a key role in SSA's electrification process highlights the importance of planning for the power system accordingly. While most industrialised countries now face the issue of integrating renewables into existing power grids, in large parts of SSA the opportunity is there to build whole new networks that can directly cope with high shares of variable—and decentralised—renewable power generation.

It is noteworthy that emerging economies—with China and India at the forefront—are effectively leading the global renewable energy transition by showing the boldest commitment to wind and solar development (REN21 2017). This increases prospects for south-south cooperation and trade, which should bring higher availability and affordability of equipment as well as accumulated experience in renewable energy policy and business in the context of developing energy markets. In this context, SSA is set to play a central role as global supplier of raw materials—and rare minerals in particular—which is something that opens up opportunities but also risks, particularly in fragile countries (Box 3.1).

Box 3.1: SSA's Rare Minerals

One of the enabling conditions for variable renewables is storage. Globally, there is quite a lot of uncertainty around the future of utility-scale batteries, however as of today lithium-ion solutions (i.e. the same type that powers smartphones and electric cars) seem to be the preferred solution, even though their appropriateness for grid applications is often questioned (Industrial Minerals 2016). The global boom for these batteries—which is expected to skyrocket as key global economies like China and the EU are taking drastic steps towards e-mobility—is driving demand of the often rare minerals that are required to produce them, like lithium, cobalt, nickel, and many more.

This goes hand in hand with the demand of rare minerals for the production of PV, and even wind turbines. Several analysts predict that the new geopolitics of energy in the era of renewables will be built around these minerals, and point out that the global relevance of SSA production is already evident. Notably, the Democratic Republic of Congo is the biggest cobalt supplier in the world, and Zimbabwe is a key global producer of lithium and copper. In many cases, human rights abuse and environmental damage are common in these mines, and while the problem is well known, the global demand is so high (and for some materials, reserves are so rare) that buyers mostly turn a blind eye on them (Levin Sources 2017).

More initiatives from the demand side are needed (e.g. the Responsible Cobalt Initiative), but it is also critical that African governments themselves take a greater hold of their mineral wealth (including through legislation, and regionally coordinated action) to avoid the draining of SSA's rare minerals in exchange of a little payback.

3.1 Solar

The potential of solar energy in Africa is naturally high. The continent is located between latitudes 37°N and 32°S and spans a vast area that crosses the equator and both tropics. African countries receive a very high number of annual sunshine hours and the average solar irradiation is quite fairly distributed (though areas of Sahara, Sahel, the south-west tip of the continent and the horn of Africa are exceptionally sunny). This means that policy and financial restrictions aside, solar technologies could supply heat and power to virtually everyone, even the most remote communities.

Options for power generation from solar energy include utility-size PV (conventional or concentrated photovoltaic) and CSP (concentrated solar thermal power) as well as small-scale PV systems suitable for off-grid power generation. Figures 3.1 and 3.2 show the distribution of Global Horizontal Irradiation (GHI) and Direct Normal Irradiation (DNI) in the subcontinent, respectively. The first one is commonly used as a reference of solar potential in general, as it sums direct and diffuse solar radiation, while the second one (i.e. its direct component) is indicative of CSP potential in particular (Box 3.2). While for PV there is no real lower applicability threshold—the feasibility of a project rather depends on the technology used and the specific design of the installation, in fact PV is also applicable at higher latitudes and colder climates—a CSP plant requires direct sun rays and a clear sky—so for CSP, deserts present ideal natural conditions.

Box 3.2: Estimating the Potential of Distributed Renewable Resources

Since renewable sources are highly distributed in nature (especially solar and wind), there are a number of physical limitations to be taken into account when estimating their technical potential and in turn their economic feasibility. Natural characteristics of irradiation, wind speed etc. can only be taken as a starting point for the evaluation of the suitability of a given technology.

There is a growing body of knowledge on the potential use of Geographic Information System (GIS) tools for renewable energy infrastructure planning and—particularly for Africa—electrification pathways. The basic procedure to come up with a geographical representation of renewable potential is the following: first, collecting data on the physical availability of resource (spatial distribution), then excluding zones that are not suitable for building infrastructure (e.g. water bodies, protected areas, etc.), finally determining a maximum limit to the distance from centres of consumption (e.g. cities) and existing grid infrastructure. Additional information of various nature can result in further geographical constraints, the establishment of priority areas (e.g. decentralised productive uses), coefficients to be applied (e.g. efficiency of production, power distribution losses), etc. A similar procedure can be adopted for determining the potential for biofuels but it has to take into account land use with a higher degree of detail.

It should be noted that such procedure is subject to a variety of assumptions and approximations (sometimes due to a heavy reliance on aggregated satellite data), which may result in overestimations or conservative assessments. This means that large scale maps—like those included in this book—need further processing in order to produce accurate estimates or to serve for real project siting. For the purpose of this book we only aim at giving a sense of magnitude of resource endowment, reporting estimates made by international organization such as the International Renewable Energy Agency and the World Bank, and inviting the interested reader to look for more detail in specialized literature.

Other than power, solar energy can be used to produce heat for domestic uses or non-intensive industrial activities (like textile that use low-to-medium process temperatures) as well as cooling (critical for remote hospitals and clinics). Crucially for rural communities, agricultural uses of solar (heat and power) include irrigation, food processing, and storage, and both CSP and PV technologies can bring desalination and wastewater treatment to communities where fresh water is scarce.

All these possible uses make solar technologies attractive for a number of sectors from energy generation, to agriculture, and water supply. The main limitations of solar technologies are relatively high costs—especially for CSP—and access to finance.

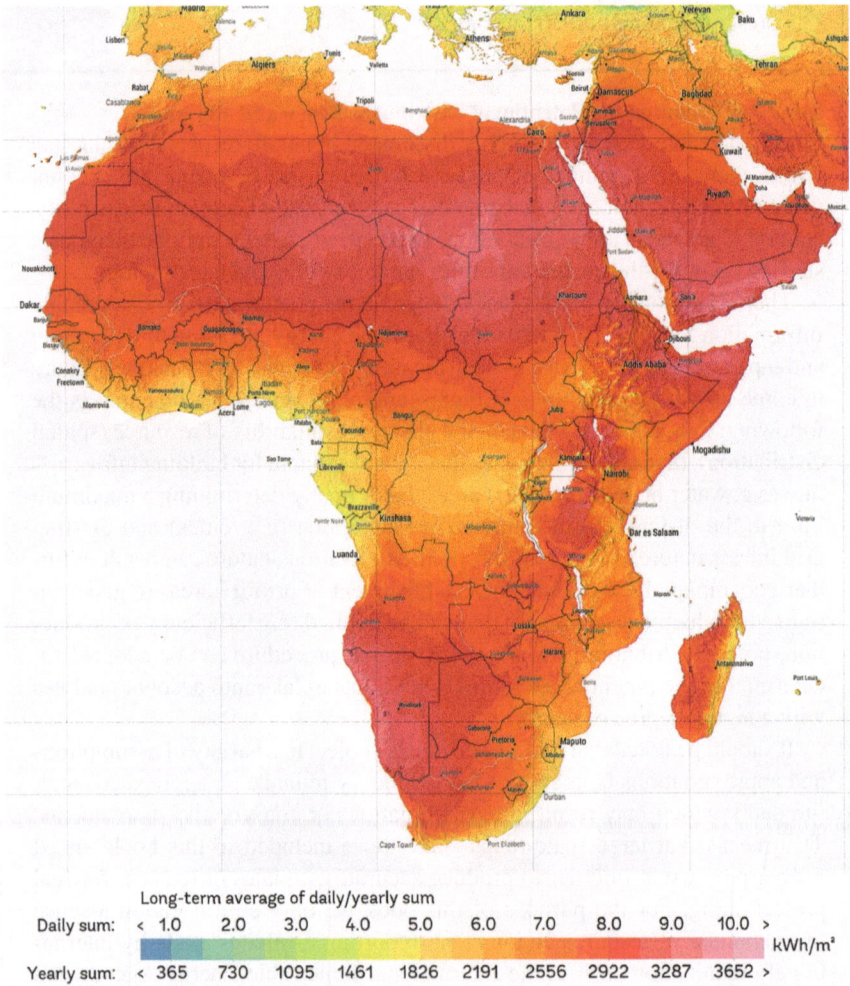

Fig. 3.1 Solar energy potential. Global horizontal irradiation. *Source* Global Solar Atlas, owned by the World Bank Group and provided by Solargis

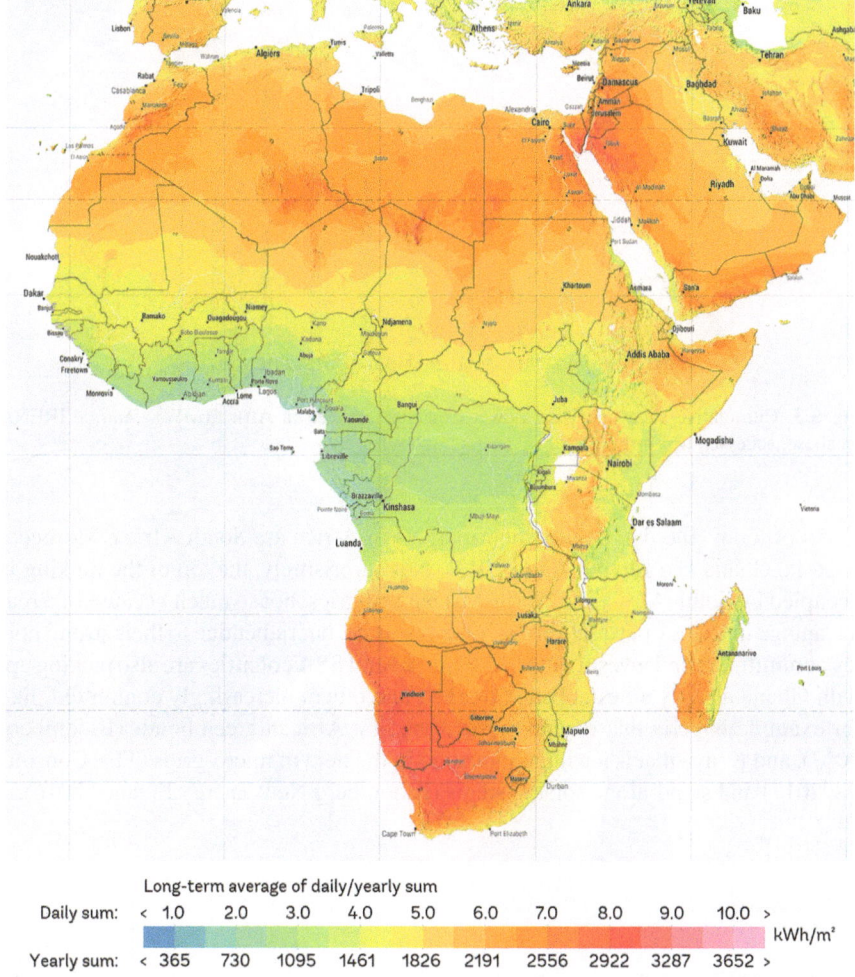

Fig. 3.2 Solar CSP energy potential. Direct normal irradiation. *Source* Global Solar Atlas, owned by the World Bank Group and provided by Solargis

Still, we are already witnessing a non-negligible rise in the deployment of solar largely driven by quickly falling prices of PV equipment.

The power capacity built in the past ten years consists of both large-scale plants (PV and CSP) and small scale (PV) (Fig. 3.3). While the latter represents a small share of the total capacity added, it is important to underline that PV-powered stand-alone systems and mini-grids are becoming the most popular (and cheapest) way of producing electricity far from the grid, and it is expected that off-grid rural electrification in SSA will be driven specifically by this technology (International Energy Agency 2017).

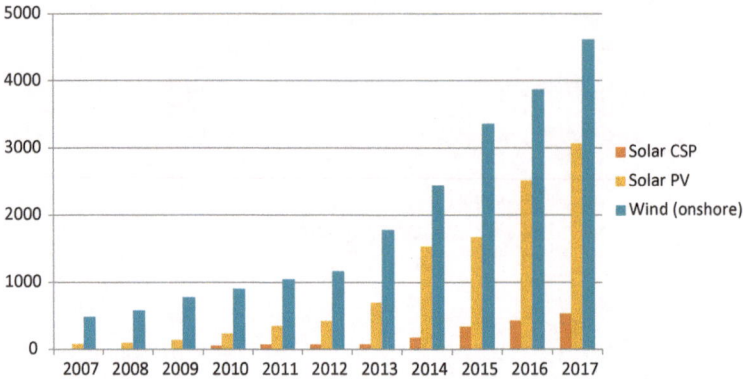

Fig. 3.3 Cumulative solar and wind power capacity installed in Africa (MW). *Source* IRENA database, accessed in April 2018

As of today, the five largest solar markets in Africa are South Africa, Morocco, Algeria, Ghana and Egypt (Tiyou 2017). Not surprisingly, the top of the ranking is occupied by South Africa and North African countries, not so much because of a real advantage in terms of availability of solar resource, but rather due to their strong policy commitment and investments. However several SSA countries are also picking up, with Ghana already an established market, and others increasingly committed, like for example Nigeria that recently issued the first African green bonds (Bloomberg 2017), and Kenya that is leading innovation in the field of micro-grids (TFE Consulting 2017) and stand-alone solar systems (Bloomberg New Energy Finance 2016).

3.2 Wind

Mechanical energy from wind turbines can be used to power a variety of mechanisms, like pumps for irrigation, or to produce electricity. While wind mills can be central assets for rural communities—and indeed they are widely used in some countries—here we talk about wind power turbines because of their potential to accelerate electrification in SSA. This means both large scale projects and small scale installations, which can be an integral part of a mini-grid together with solar PV, for example.

Compared to solar potential, wind potential is less fairly distributed across the continent. The main factor determining the geography of wind potential is wind speed, in turn highly dependent on pressure gradients and the shape of the landscape. Hence the presence of deserts, coastlines, and natural channels, all play in favour of high wind speeds. In Africa, the best wind quality can be found in the rugged regions of Sahara and Sahel (all countries, including the most central Niger, Chad, and Sudan), along the coast, and in mountainous areas of Southern Africa (particularly

South Africa, Lesotho, Malawi, Zambia), and in some parts of East Africa, especially
in the horn of Africa and along the Great Rift Valley (Eritrea, Djibouti, Somalia,
Ethiopia, Kenya, Tanzania) (International Renewable Energy Agency 2015).

The wind power density (a function of wind speed) showed in Fig. 3.4 is a measure of wind potential at a given height: here 100 m from the ground. As a rule
of thumb 150–250 W/m^2 can be considered a fair value of wind power density,
250–350 W/m^2 is good, and over 350 W/m^2 is excellent (Renewable Energy Science
and Technology). While this type of map is not suitable for project siting—other factors can significantly change the estimate at higher resolutions and using direct wind
measurements—it gives a first indication of the varying potential of wind across the
continent.

Similar to solar, we can observe an exponential growth of wind power capacity
installed in Africa in the past ten years (Fig. 3.3) and point at the biggest five wind
power markets that are driving this growth. They are South Africa, Morocco, Egypt,
Ethiopia, and Kenya. Again, it is the strong commitment of these countries to renewable energy policy that is making a difference. Among these, Ethiopia and Kenya are
relatively new players, the latter entering the ranks of top African wind producers
with one single massive project (the already mentioned Lake Turkana, see Box 3.3),
and the first with a number of smaller schemes that aim explicitly at working in
tandem with hydropower production, given a lucky complementarity between dry
seasons with higher wind potentials and wet seasons with higher hydro potential
(Tiyou 2016).

Box 3.3: Lake Turkana Wind Power

Lake Turkana in Kenya is a very ambitious renewable projects: once com-
pleted, it will be the largest wind farm in Africa (310 MW of planned power
capacity) and the largest single private investment in the history of Kenya (623
million euros) (African Development Bank 2014). However the project is also
located in one of the poorest areas of the country. The wind turbines will be
built scattered across a vast area (162 km^2 of which 0.02% will be physically
occupied by the farm's facilities) that is a dry-season vegetation buffer for
pastoralists, and this has sparked significant opposition to the project since its
inception, which culminated in a legal lawsuit for lack of transparency in the
procedure of land rights acquisition (Kamadi 2016; Critical Resource 2016).

As for the Lake Turkana project, many other potential wind and geothermal
sites in Kenya practically overlap with areas that are vital for indigenous
people, who are often nomadic and live in "community lands" (forests, grazing
areas, and shrines) (Sena 2015). In fact, land tenure issues are a common reality
for many large-scale renewable energy projects planned all over rural Africa
and it is one that should not be ignored, given the potential conflict they could
end up sparking.

The project in Lake Turkana is now moving forward with a particular
emphasis on community engagement and consultation (and minimum fencing

of land areas) (Lake Turkana Wind Power). The experience from this project shows that the development of large renewable energy projects in SSA put both developers and institutions in front of the need to ensure transparency and accountability—also as a means to manage investment risks.

In Africa, all of the wind power installed is found onshore because offshore solutions are generally more expensive (in fact, almost all of the offshore wind globally installed is located in Europe). However, it should be noted that offshore wind is generally associated with higher yields, and that the global industry is expanding (International Renewable Energy Agency 2016). Though at present there is a relative lack of offshore wind speed data to allow for a geospatial assessment of offshore wind potential in Africa (Mentis et al. 2015), it is clear that this resource is an asset to be considered by coastal countries (see for instance a feasibility assessment for a site in Nigeria (Effiom et al. 2016)).

Other offshore renewable energy technologies could also represent an asset in the future (e.g. wave energy, which theoretical potential in Africa is estimated at 3,500 TWh/year), however for now almost all of the technologies available to harness them are still at a conceptual phase of development and the global capacity installed today is negligible (Lewis et al. 2011). The only exception is tidal energy, which can be harnessed by underwater turbines and indeed one such project has been recently proposed in Ghana (CNN 2017).

3.3   Hydropower

Hydropower plants can be classified by the amount of capacity they produce or by the characteristics of infrastructural components of the single plant. For the sake of simplicity, here we distinguish only between large and small hydropower, meaning projects that give a major or minor contribution to power generation capacity and have a major or minor impact on water flows.[1] In reality, when it comes to water flow alteration, what makes a difference is the presence or absence of a dam or reservoir. Hydropower plants with little or no water accumulation are called run-of river. Most small hydropower plants are run-of river, but also some large ones, as long as they can count on high and stable flows like those of many tropical rivers. A plant counting on one upper and one lower dam can also serve as "pump-storage", sending water up when there is a surplus of energy and releasing it when needed to supply peak-loads of demand.

Different sizes and types of hydropower plants bring about different issues, but overall large projects that exert a strong control on water and sediment flows have the biggest environmental impact. For very large water flows like those of some

---

[1] Technically, a hydropower plant is considered large starting from a minimum of 100 MW, medium between 20 and 100 MW, and small from 1 and 20 MW (and mini, micro and pico for progressively lower capacities).

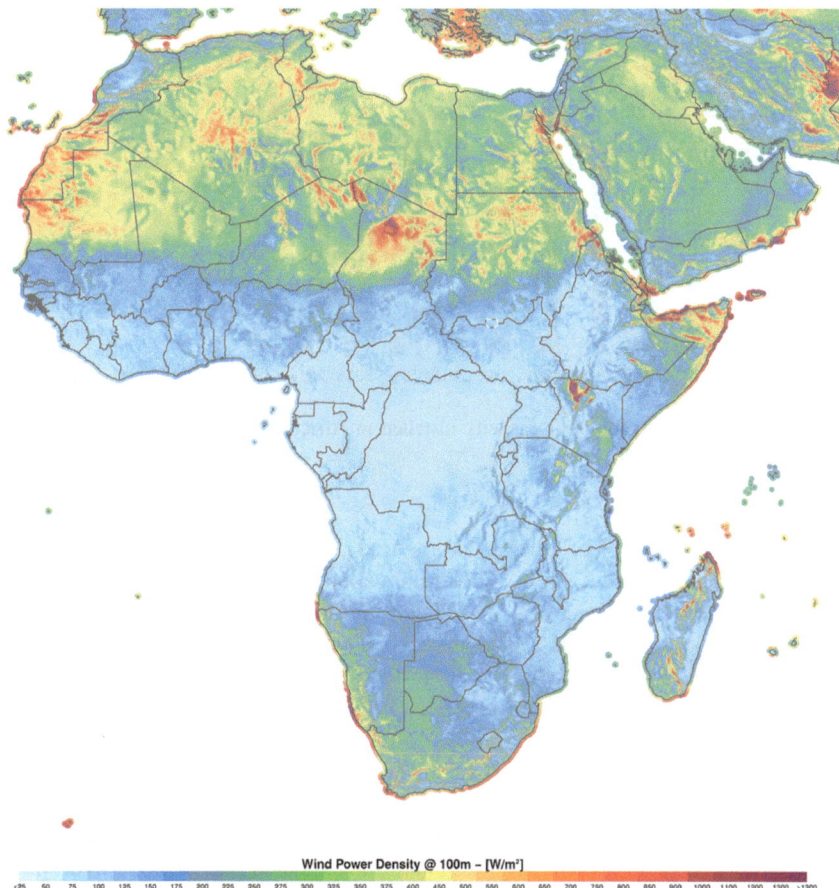

Fig. 3.4 Distribution of wind energy: wind power density (W/m2) at 100 m elevation. *Source* Global Wind Atlas 2.0, a free, web-based application developed, owned and operated by the Technical University of Denmark (DTU) in partnership with the World Bank Group, utilizing data provided by Vortex, with funding provided by the Energy Sector Management Assistance Program (ESMAP)

African rivers, we are talking about mega projects with capacities of hundreds, if not thousands of MW (i.e. GW). Such projects raise high hopes for broad electrification, but they are also the most controversial and expensive ones.

With its major river basins (Congo, Nile, Senegal, Niger, Zambesi, Volta, Orange), SSA is endowed with a huge hydropower potential and the Congo basin alone—the largest in terms of water discharge—counts for 40% of the total. Most of the potential is found in Central Africa (Congo, Democratic Republic of Congo, Cameroon), but estimates are also noteworthy in East Africa (Ethiopia), Southern Africa (Angola, Mozambique, Madagascar) and West Africa (Guinea, Nigeria, Senegal).

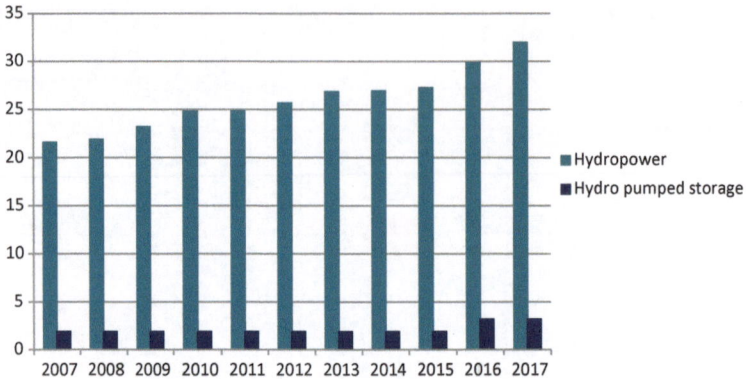

Fig. 3.5 Cumulative hydropower capacity installed in Africa (GW). *Source* IRENA database, accessed in April 2018

There is a huge gap between this potential and actual hydropower production in SSA: of the estimated 280 GW potential capacity, only 10% is currently tapped (International Energy Agency 2014). While Central Africa has the largest technically feasible hydro potential (570,730 GWh/year), it also has the lowest rate of utilization of this potential (3%). For comparison, North Africa has about one tenth of the technical potential of Central Africa (59,693 GWh/year) but produces a higher amount of hydropower.

Still—in Africa like in the rest of the world—hydropower is the most widely utilized renewable energy source. The total hydropower installed capacity in Africa is about ten times that of solar or wind, with new investments advancing with a more or less constant growth (Fig. 3.5) and it is expected that by 2030 hydropower will overtake coal as the fuel with the highest share of power production in the subcontinent (International Energy Agency 2017).

3.3.1 Large Hydropower

It is easy to understand the appeal of large hydropower for African countries that have the potential to develop it (see Table 3.3). Hydropower can produce a significant and steady supply of electricity, using an indigenous and renewable source, and counting on a well-established, low-carbon technology. Working as a baseload power source, it can serve the demand of cities and industrial areas. All of this at a relatively low cost: as of today hydropower still constitutes the cheapest option for electricity production on large scale in Africa (International Renewable Energy Agency 2018). Furthermore, the construction of a dam can serve multiple purposes including water supply, which in some areas is urgently needed to alleviate pressing issues of low access to water, sanitation, and irrigation.

Table 3.3 Hydropower capacity in countries where the total (installed and planned) is higher than 1 GW

Country	MW in operation	MW planned
Angola	1,346	5,639
Cameroon	736	10,784
Congo	287	14,090
Democratic Republic of Congo	2,398	47,361
Egypt	2,866	2,143
Ethiopia	3,812	25,570
Equatorial Guinea	120	920
Gabon	324	1,553
Ghana	1,580	554
Guinea	347	3,138
Ivory Coast	599	1,023
Kenya	818	1,313
Lesotho	73	1,204
Liberia	64	2,593
Malawi	349	661
Morocco	1,795	654
Mozambique	2,181	5,560
Nigeria	2,044	8,990
South Africa	3,554	20
South Sudan	0	2,147
Sudan	1,733	1,965
Tanzania	561	5,489
Uganda	630	2,726
Zambia	1,900	3,505
Zimbabwe	750	3,096

Source Author's elaboration on International Journal for Hydropower and Dams, 2017

All these reasons historically determined the fortune of large hydropower, as can be seen by looking at the number of African countries that rely on it for the biggest part of their generation: in many SSA countries the share of hydro in the electricity generation mix is significant, and can be as high as 99.9%. This is the case of Mozambique, Democratic Republic of Congo, and Zambia. (World Bank) (Fig. 3.6).

Today, the future of large hydropower is rather uncertain. Although it is clear that its characteristics make it perfect, in theory, to reach the twofold objective of increasing large-scale power capacity while balancing an increasing share of renewables, African hydropower developers are facing some practical challenges.

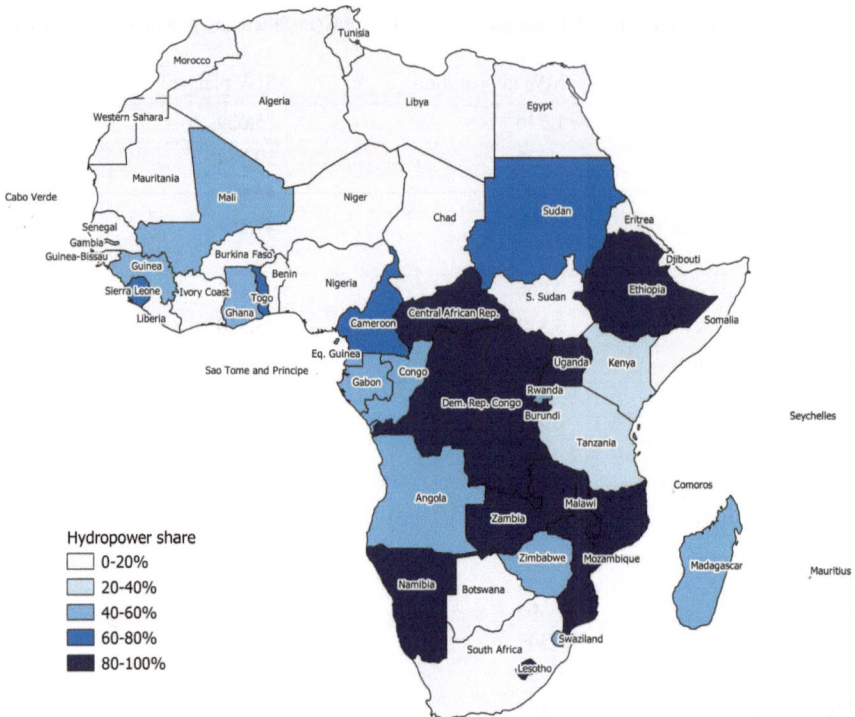

Fig. 3.6 Country dependency on hydropower. *Source* Author's elaboration with data from the International Energy Agency database, accessed in April 2018

The first is that there is an increasing public opposition to hydropower, particularly due to the environmental and social impact of large and mega dams, both on site and at transboundary level. Hydropower dams may require flooding large land areas, potentially displacing communities and reducing temporarily the flow of water available for other uses downstream, such as agriculture. In SSA these issues are particularly pressing: large shares of population count on the direct use of water resources for their livelihoods, and all countries rely to some extent on shared water resources (Grey 2002). It should be noted that the environmental impact of very large projects can be as far-reaching as to compromise ecosystems of global importance, such as the "Congo Plume", a major global carbon sink formed by the discharge of the Congo river in the Atlantic Ocean, threatened by the Grand Inga Dam project.

The second is the adverse impact of climate change, and rainfall variability, on hydropower generation. Several African countries are already experiencing severe power disruption as a result of low water levels in lakes and reservoirs. Major shortages recently hit for instance the huge Cahora Bassa in Mozambique (Bloomberg 2016), the Kenyan Sondu-Miriu and Masinga (Reuters 2017a), and Lake Malawi (Reuters 2017b). Over-reliance on hydropower adds to the weight of rain-fed agriculture in tying the economic performance of SSA economies to changes in rainfall levels (in contrast, for instance, with North African ones) (Barrios Cobos et al. 2008). From this perspective it is clear that not only needs the hydropower sector to adapt to climate change, but also the broader energy system has to diversify (Conway et al. 2017).

Last but not least there is the issue of funding, as these projects require large sums of upfront capital. Domestic markets may be too small to justify large investments, and at the same time poor regional interconnections remain a major impediment to the possibility of export. Nevertheless, since large hydropower remains a strategic resource for many countries, the sector is capable of mobilizing massive funds from a multitude of global, regional, and local investors. Notably the African Development Bank—i.e. the executing agency of the Programme for Infrastructure Development in Africa PIDA—explicitly supports hydropower as part of regional grid expansion projects aimed at the improvement of regional power pools.

It should be noted that due to often limited availability of public money, the hydropower sector receives significant funds from foreign lenders (most importantly China). In SSA, they may have a competitive advantage over multilateral development banks, who are bound to increasingly strict requirements that make them less reliable and more expensive than other lenders (this is the case of the World Bank that, after more or less a decade of stall in the 90s re-engaged with large hydropower in Africa but only after updating their standards and guidelines on social and environmental impact) (International Rivers 2013).

The most discussed mega projects in Africa today are the Great Renaissance Ethiopian Dam (GERD), under construction—which is already increasing transboundary tensions with Egypt—and the proposed Grand Inga on the Congo river—which, if built in its entire extent, would establish itself as the largest centre of power production in the world, in terms of capacity twice as big as the Chinese Three Gorges (see Box 3.3).

Box 3.3 Grand Inga

The big hydropower story of SSA is certainly represented by the Grand Inga Dam, a proposed hydropower dam complex on the Congo River at Inga Falls, in the Democratic Republic of Congo. This project, first envisaged by the Belgians in the 1950s, would alone have a capacity of 44 GW—a potential game-changer of the overall SSA's electricity scenario. Under the dictatorship of Mobutu Sésé Seko, the first two phases of the complex (Inga 1 and Inga 2) were constructed, totalling a combined capacity of 1.7 GW that still today represents a large share of the country's total installed capacity (2.5 GW). Over the last decades, the country has sought to further advance the Grand Inga Dam project. However, the project has systematically been delayed. Most recently, the government has fast-tracked the advancement of the third dam of the complex (Inga 3, with a projected capacity of 4.8 GW). In 2014, the World Bank approved a USD 73-million grant for the technical preparation of the project. However, it suspended this grant in 2016, as a result of a 'different strategic direction' taken by the government (World Bank 2016). The choppy development of the Grand Inga Dam project is an illustration of how difficult it is to advance large hydropower projects in SSA.

3.3.2 Small Hydropower

Small hydropower can be a key element of local development, because its production is stable enough to supply an industrial activity for the benefit of surrounding communities (notably in terms of irrigation and electrification). Of all off-grid options small hydro has the lowest electricity generation price, and it is probably the easiest to design, operate, and maintain. While not comparable to that of mega dams, the environmental impact of small hydropower is not negligible. Together, numerous small installations can bring major hydro-morphologic alterations to river courses as well as changes to habitats and land use, making production unsuitable to protected and biodiversity-rich areas.

Africa as a whole has an estimated small hydropower potential of 12,197 MW and some countries are particularly rich of it, namely Kenya, Ethiopia, Mozambique, Ghana, Angola, Cameroon and Nigeria (Fig. 3.7). Less than 5% of this potential (580 MW) is exploited and the countries with the highest utilization rates are once again South Africa and the North African region (UN Industrial Development Organization and International Center on Small Hydro Power 2016).

Small hydro infrastructure from the time of the colonies can still be found in several countries, although very often such schemes have fallen out of use due to aging, unaffordability of maintenance costs, or lack of interest from institutions (Othieno and Awange 2016).

3.4 Geothermal

Geothermal plants convert heat into electricity, using steam that is naturally stored underground. While deep heat resources are available everywhere, in some areas—near volcanoes, geologic rifts, and hot springs—they are more easily accessible. From the perspective of power generation, this technology has the key advantage of being dispatchable, which makes it a good complement to intermittent renewable power. Having said that, thanks to its low variable costs, geothermal is typically used to provide base load power.

Africa's known geothermal potential is concentrated in the East Africa, in the geologically active area of the Great Rift Valley, which extends from Djibouti to

Fig. 3.7 Map of small
hydropower potential (MW).
Source The World Small
Hydropower Development
Report 2016. UN Industrial
Development Organization
and International Center on
Small Hydro Power 2016

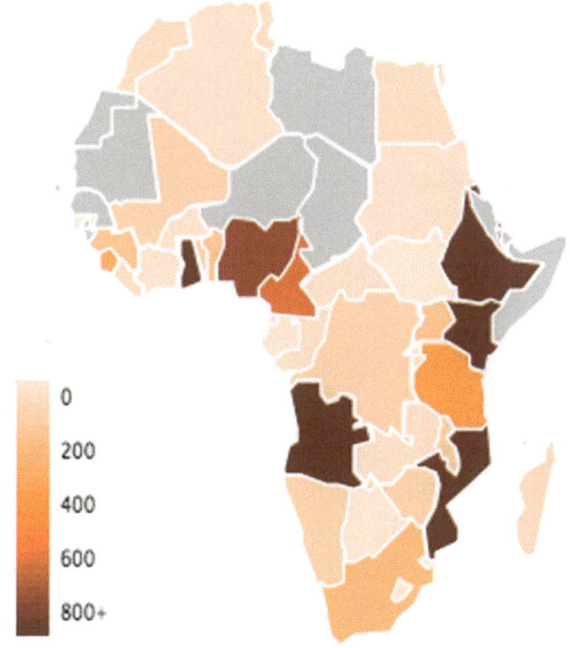

Mozambique (Fig. 3.8). The total potential geothermal capacity in Africa is estimated to be around 15 GW, of which only 0.6% is currently exploited. Almost all of the geothermal power installed is found in Kenya (600 MW) that grew in the past decade to become a global leader in the sector (REN21 2017; Think Geo Energy 2017). It is noteworthy that becoming the predominant source of energy in the country, geothermal has significantly increased the drought resilience of the Kenyan power sector, once over-reliant on hydropower.

Neighbouring Ethiopia also started harnessing its geothermal potential and is aiming at reaching 1 GW capacity in 2021 (Reuters 2017c), while others are more or less actively pursuing geothermal exploration and drilling. This is an expensive and economically risky process that has much in common with oil and gas exploration, in the sense that the exact potential of a geothermal site can only be known once the drilling has taken place (although unlike with oil and gas, electricity generation needs to happen on site because the steam cannot be stored and transported, potentially adding to the cost of project the element of long-distance transmission lines). This means that geothermal developers need significant support in terms of risk management from governments and donors (ESI Africa 2016).

As for solar, geothermal energy can also be used directly in industries that need heat at low temperatures (e.g. the flower industry in Kenya) although it is clear that in most places such direct uses may not be viable, and too complex. Geothermal can supply heat pumps for residential cooling and hot water production—and the current technology can potentially evolve into off-grid power generation (Richter

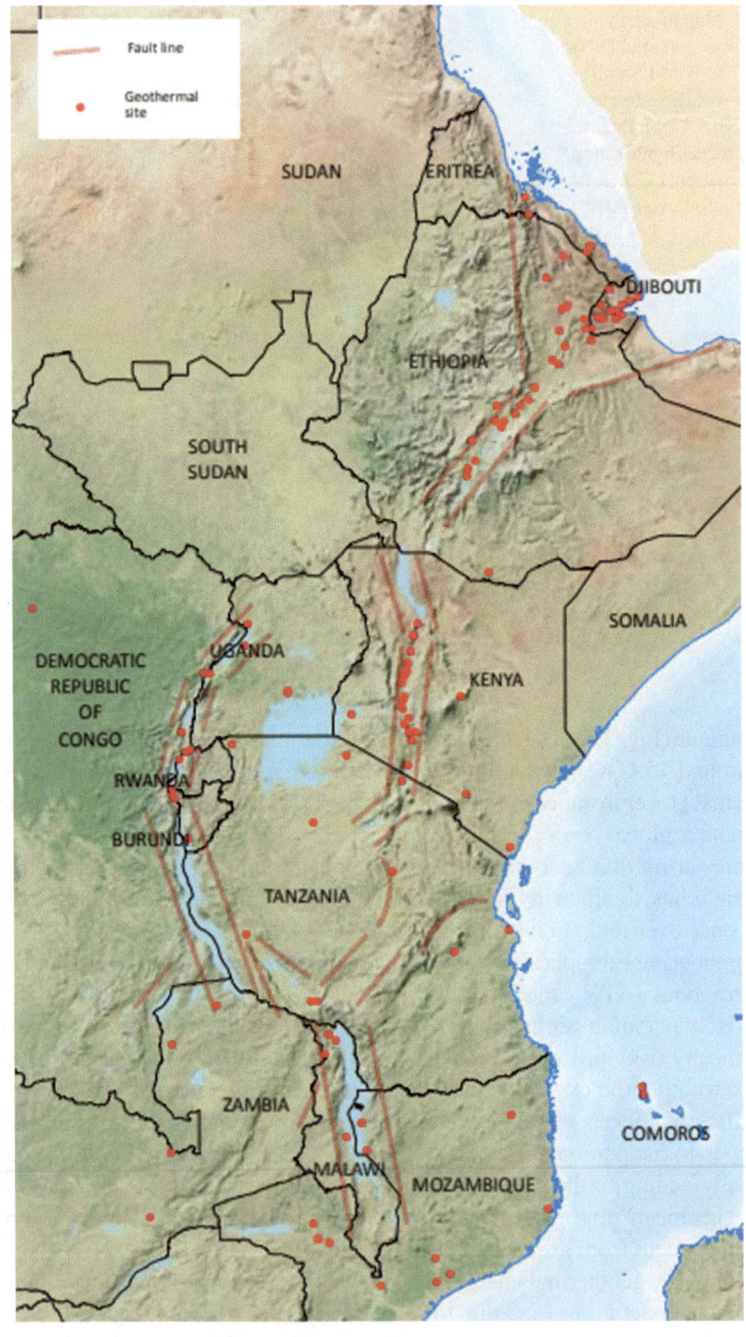

◄**Fig. 3.8** Geothermal potential sites in East Africa. *Source* Atlas of Africa energy resources (African Development Bank et al. 2017)

2016). Although these technologies are not yet widespread in Africa, it is easy to imagine that these could sustainably supply the increasing demand for heating and cooling of East Africa's growing cities.

3.5 Modern Bioenergy: Efficiency, Waste Valorisation, and Biofuels

Bioenergy can refer to heat, power, or a combination of them (Combined Heat and Power: CHP) produced from biomass. The initial feedstock can be processed to various degrees into usable solid, liquid, or gaseous fuels (e.g. pellets, charcoal, biofuels, biogas), however in Africa it is still overwhelmingly combusted directly, either for cooking purposes (and concurrently for heating and lighting) or, to a lesser extent, for industrial processes.

Figure 3.9 shows the percentage of tree cover on African land. During the past century, the consumption of wood has been steadily increasing in Africa and it is expected to keep on doing so, despite the efforts being made to reduce it. This adds pressure to forests that are often already threatened by deforestation due to urbanization and expansion of agricultural land (Africa Renewable Energy Access Program (AFREA) 2011).

As discussed (Chap. 2) the problem of widespread, inefficient use of solid biomass in households is linked to a number of factors, among which poverty and the geographical remoteness of rural population are only the most evident, hence the challenge of switching to efficient, clean, and environmentally sustainable[2] biomass use is not trivial. A multitude of opportunities exist and there are virtuous examples of innovation in Africa, though they are most often limited to local entrepreneurship instead of being part of wider, modern bioenergy policies. For wood and charcoal, the primary policy objective (besides fuel switching) is twofold: increasing the efficiency of combustion on the user side, and building sustainable value chains on the production side. The potential here is huge but policy efforts need to play out at many different levels, from the support to local markets for efficient cookstoves and high-efficiency fuels, all the way up to sustainable forest management. Considering that the wood and charcoal market in Africa employs tens-to-hundreds thousands of people, such policies could have a massive impact on rural development (Africa Renewable Energy Access Program (AFREA) 2011; GIZ 2014).

---

[2]Establishing the sustainability of biomass production is necessary to be able to determine if biomass can be considered "renewable". Statistics are inaccurate however, and this forces analysts to take arbitrary assumptions, like considering industrial uses of biomass as sustainable as opposed to traditional cooking with solid biomass (International Renewable Energy Agency 2015).

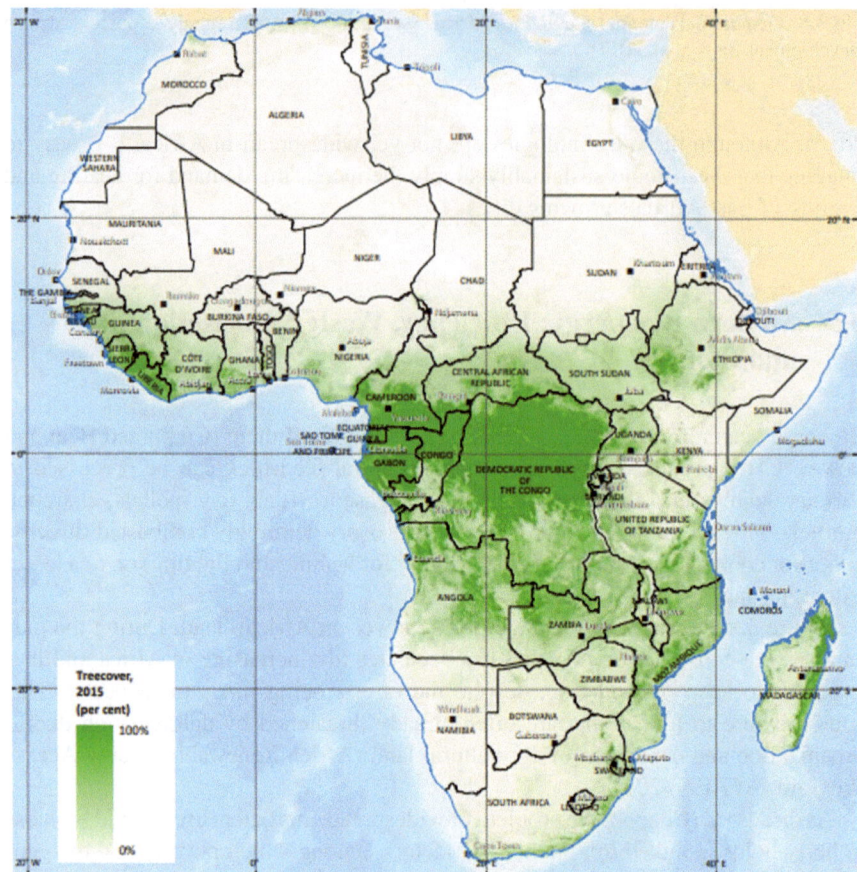

Fig. 3.9 Percentage of tree cover in Africa. *Source* Atlas of Africa energy resources (African Development Bank et al. 2017)

A large potential for bioenergy comes from waste and residues of various nature. Biomass and waste already provide around 30% of the thermal energy used in African industry (the rest coming from fossil fuels) but only 8% of this can be considered "modern"—in the sense that it is processed from residues that would otherwise be disposed of. In SSA, bagasse (i.e. the main byproduct of sugarcane processing) is the most commonly utilised feedstock for CHP production. Indeed, for sugarcane producing countries (e.g. Mauritius, South Africa, Egypt, Sudan, Kenya, Swaziland and Zimbabwe) bagasse can be really valuable as the cases of Mauritius and South Africa show, where sugarcane producers already produce more electricity than needed to cover their own industrial demand, selling their surplus to the national grid. CHP production holds significant potential also when it comes to the residues of wood processing and logging (IRENA estimates a total of 20 GW of potential power generation capacity from this sector), however this type of bioenergy is not yet widely adopted and there are only a few wood based power plants (about a dozen) scattered across the continent (International Renewable Energy Agency 2015).

When it comes to municipal waste, the potential in SSA is massive and so far basically unexploited. On large scales, valorising waste is not only a means of advancing renewables and energy efficiency, but also a clever way of solving the huge problem of waste disposal. Ethiopia seems to be leading the way, having recently announced the construction of the first waste-to power plant in the continent (UN Environment Program 2017). Considering the speed of urbanization in Africa it is clear that this type of solution will have a role to play in the future of many countries.

There are several open questions around the sustainability of bioenergy and its potential as a global climate mitigation solution. However, when it comes to SSA specifically, at least two considerations appear to be quite straightforward. First, as African forests are severely threatened, modernizing the bioenergy value chain (and adding value to the sector) could significantly contribute to better protect them. Second, given the importance of African forests as global carbon sinks, there are opportunities to value bioenergy efforts in the context of the UN Reducing Emissions from Deforestation and Forest Degradation (REDD+) support program—provided that they reduce pressure on forests or contribute to increase forested areas (Bertzky et al. 2012). Such opportunities could be further enhanced by appropriately recognizing REDD + efforts as carbon credits in international carbon markets (Bosetti et al. 2011).

The potential of using biofuels (e.g. bioethanol and biodiesel) in the transport sector of SSA countries is also significant. Biofuels can be first-generation, if the feedstock comes from crops that in some way end up competing with food production (e.g. vegetable oils, sugarcane), otherwise they are second- (e.g. bagasse, wood, waste) or third-generation (i.e. algae). As anticipated, estimating the potential of biofuels (particularly first-generation) is not an easy task: it is clear that the production of fuel crops in SSA, where malnutrition is widespread and food insecurity sometimes translates into famine, can be a very sensitive topic. Still, the potential can be estimated taking into account land competition. Methodologies may vary but some assessments are quite encouraging. IRENA estimates for instance that by 2050 liquid biofuels could meet and even exceed the fuel demand from the transport sector of Ghana, Mozambique, Nigeria, South Africa and Uganda, provided that dedicated policies are set up (International Renewable Energy Agency 2017a). All in all, the employment of biofuels as transport fuels would require a considerable effort from the side of policy makers because they compete with oil (and to a certain extent gas) that is a much better established and often subsidised (hence more competitive) option.

Finally, a special mention should go to biogas, as it valorizes waste-type feedstock and is highly versatile on the user side, hence it can be safely used for cooking. A product of the anaerobic digestion of organic materials, it can be produced from a variety of free (or low-cost) sources such as animal manure, agricultural residues, wastewater sludge, and municipal waste. Depending on the size, digesters can serve industrial uses as well as residential complexes. Once compressed, biogas can also be used for transport. In SSA, the technical potential of domestic biogas for cooking in rural households and for agro-industrial uses is substantial, and small-scale biogas production is already starting to take ground across the continent, particularly in Kenya and Ethiopia (REN21 2017).

3.6   Upscaling Renewables

This chapter so far showed that the potential for renewable development in Africa is as high as diversified, but also that harnessing it requires a dedicated effort. Given the potential renewable power and the broader benefits that electrification brings (Chap. 2), the next paragraphs look specifically at the challenges of upscaling renewables in the power sector. Considerations on upscaling clean cooking solutions are more scattered throughout the book, including at the end of Chap. 5.

Not all countries can count on the same renewable sources, and some of them are unpredictable, or highly variable over time (e.g. daily, seasonally). This means that the development of renewables has to be planned in a way that maximises generation where the single resources are available, balancing at the same time their variability at the level of the grid.

The variability of renewable loads can be forecasted and subsequently managed by acting on the supply side (i.e. building up a reliable mix of technologies, introducing storage, or designing hybrid power plants) as well as on the demand side (e.g. through appropriate pricing schemes), while being able to respond fast to sudden interruptions at the source or unexpected peaks of demand—to avoid blackouts—may require a certain sophistication of grid management. Smart meters and fast-responding batteries may have an important role to play in this sense, although their uptake in SSA is currently constrained by the costs of equipment. As storage solutions make their first appearance (particularly for off-grid installations) and experts try to develop business models tailored to SSA utilities and users (Tsagas 2017), betting on hybrid solutions and matching complementary technologies can already go a long way to manage the variability of renewables on large scales.

One clear advantage of renewables is that they are widely distributed, which opens up opportunities for decentralised production of heat and/or power. To a certain extent, solutions can be developed fast by local entrepreneurs even without explicit governmental support for a specific technology, particularly at small scale, however it is fundamental that countries set up the most appropriate and effective policy frameworks to enable a systematic transition to modern renewables.

Comparing the experience of countries all over the world it is clear that there is no one-size-fit-all policy approach, and while the presence of some kind of framework is a prerequisite for renewable development, this may succeed or fail depending on a multitude of factors. The World Bank developed a tool called RISE (Regulatory Indicators for Sustainable Energy) to monitor specifically the status of policy frameworks to advance access to modern energy, and renewable energy in particular. Table 3.4 shows how African countries score based on a rather extensive list of aggregated indicators, namely:

Table 3.4 RISE country score for renewable energy policy framework, selected indicators (0−100)

Source World Bank, RISE website, accessed in December 2017
Note This list does not include a number of countries, for which data is not available

 (i) Legal framework for renewables (existence of a legal framework for renew-
      ables; legality of private sector ownership of generation);
 (ii) Planning for renewable expansion (existence of renewable targets and plans;
      extent of renewable energy in planning for generation as well as transmission;
      resource data and siting);
(iii) Incentives and regulatory support for renewables (existence of financial and
      regulatory incentives; transparency of legal framework; extent of grid access
      and dispatch);
 (iv) Attributes of financial and regulatory incentives (predictability, efficiency, and
      long-term sustainability);
  (v) Network connection and pricing (connection cost allocation; network usage
      and pricing; renewable grid integration);
 (vi) Counterparty risk (payment risk mitigation; public financial statements; utility
      creditworthiness);
(vii) Carbon pricing and monitoring.

At a glance, it is clear that Africa, and particularly SSA, still lags behind when
it comes to renewable policy (although it should be noted that the worst performing
indicator indicating the absence of carbon pricing mechanisms (vii) is not particularly
telling, as it simply reflects the global situation outside the OECD area).

Columns (i) and (ii) indicate that some countries lack quite basic requisites, such
as the existence of a legal framework for renewable power producers, the availability
of detailed natural resource assessments, or the presence of a clear renewable energy
policy direction. For these countries, showing policy commitment by establishing
clear targets and concrete plans for implementation is the very first step that needs
to be taken to give a positive signal to investors.

Given the massive costs required to increase power generation capacity in Africa
(see Chap. 5), the ability of governments to catalyse private funding for renewable
energy projects is crucial. As much as renewables are increasing in competitiveness,
private investors willing to develop renewable projects face significant costs and
risks, and this is true for small-scale installations as well as for projects of regional
significance. The challenge of governments is therefore to increase the confidence
of investors through policy and financial de-risking measures. The existence and
effectiveness of such measures can be seen in columns (iii), (iv), (v) and (vi).

For on-grid projects, setting up power purchase agreements (PPAs) with power
generators by ensuring that they will have access to the grid as well as a fixed long-
term price guaranteed for the power they will produce is considered a "cornerstone"
on which further policy and financial de-risking measures can build upon (Waissbein
et al. 2013). Essentially, this can be achieved with feed-in tariffs schemes (FITs) or
through auctions. The main difference is that tariffs are pre-fixed by policy makers
in the first case, while they are the result of a competitive bidding from the side of
investors in the second. Both approaches have multiple declinations and while each
one carries its own advantages and disadvantages, they can also co-exist, suggesting
that there is ample room for manoeuvre in the design of a country strategy.

Especially in SSA, the final cost for users is a critical element that can compromise the long-term sustainability of energy investments, and renewables are no exception. This means that the presence of targeted subsidies, and cross-subsidies in particular, is necessary, and as this is in turn a fiscal burden for taxpayers, it becomes vital to uncover least-cost solutions.

So while FITs have driven the first wave of renewable energy investments in Europe, auctions are enjoying more popularity in developing countries and emerging economies all over the world (International Renewable Energy Agency 2013). Compared to FITs, they stimulate competition and in turn push forward the most cost-efficient projects (Fowlie 2017). African examples of countries that successfully implemented renewable energy auctions are South Africa, Morocco, and Zambia (International Renewable Energy Agency 2017b). One of the main risks of auctions is that they tend to favour larger and well established players, potentially compromising market efficiency in the long term. While this should not be a deterrent for their implementation (it is clear that in the context of SSA the priority is to increase renewable power generation capacity) it is important that such schemes are not only carefully designed, but also monitored and, if necessary, corrected.

If auctions are proving more effective in stimulating large-scale renewable energy investments, small-scale projects seem to find better backing in FIT schemes that do not require the investor to undertake expensive tendering procedures. This is particularly important for specific target groups that have little capital but a clear motivation to produce energy, such as farmer cooperatives or small industries. It is still possible to stimulate competition among small-scale investors by topping up FIT schemes with auction-based premium payments. In Uganda for instance, the latter is assigned on the basis of technical, economic, social, and environmental performance of the company (GET FiT Uganda).

The policy support required for off-grid renewable investments and mini-grid in particular can be even more complex than for grid-connected projects. While the final goal of an enabling policy is the same—boosting private investments in the sector—in this case the market is less mature and there is much less accumulated experience of successful policies to draw from. It seems too early to expect a private sector- led growth in the mini-grid sector, and yet it is already urgent to move away from donor-led, demonstration projects that do not stimulate entrepreneurship (UN Industrial Development Organization 2017). This requires explicit government support. In general, the subsidization of mini-grids can be strategic due to the positive social impact that they can have, but it is particularly reasonable when they actually represent the least-cost electrification option (TFE Consulting 2017).

For decentralised energy the willingness and ability of consumers to pay becomes a precondition for project feasibility, which puts productive uses—industry in particular—in a key position. In mini-grids, they can guarantee a long-term purchase of power to the generator or even decide to become power producers themselves. Still, the main purpose of off-grid solutions is to accelerate access among the poorest in rural areas, and it is important to make sure that investors manage to effectively address this need elaborating targeted pro-poor business models. In this case, policy makers should aim at building up an environment where entrepreneurship can flourish and, once again, setting up the appropriate legislative frameworks and enabling access to credit are critical moves. Today, the most popular models are distributed energy service companies (DESCOs) for mini-grids, pay-as-you-go (PAYG) for stand-alone, and microfinance in general, including for the provision of cook-stoves (REN21 2017).

Being able to set up renewable energy policies and the related frameworks of implementation requires a great effort of governance. While it is important to maintain a whole-sector perspective to energy development—particularly when it comes to rural development, bioenergy, and waste recovery—renewable energy needs to be championed by appropriate institutions that have its development at the core of their mandate (i.e. Renewable Energy Authorities). As their task is both ambitious and socially significant, these organizations need to aim high in terms of objectives but also pursue transparency and accountability in the implementation of their agendas.

Good governance is also the fundamental prerequisite to get the bilateral and multilateral funding needed to develop large infrastructure projects. Especially when it comes to hydropower, international agreements will be needed to underpin water allocation agreements and, potentially, to define the roles of each country in financing and managing infrastructure. In general (independently form the technology) regional cooperation involving inter-state agreements can make large projects viable by aggregating demand to the level necessary for a viable commercial case for investment. It also offers opportunities to share the output and benefits among countries to address electricity supply deficits and support economic development.

In the long term, the possibility of manufacturing renewable energy equipment in the African continent for local and/or regional markets should be seriously considered (the cost of importing technology from overseas is significant, if not prohibitive for some countries) as well as strategic investments into assembling, operation and maintenance, and research and development (UNIDO 2017). It is important to underline that manufacturing of renewables does not refer to PV panels and wind turbines only: there is also an important unmet demand for less expensive equipment for biomass thermal power units, hydro turbines, and even clean cookstoves. Building a stronger renewable sector is also instrumental to the uptake of technological innovation. An interesting example is advanced thermal storage using molten salt batteries, an option that is particularly suitable for solar CSP and that is already a reality in South Africa and Morocco (Deign 2017).

African universities and research institutions are best positioned to develop the most appropriate technologies for the realities of the African continent. Because of its potential to stimulate local employment, the research and development of renewable energy technologies and the promotion of public-private initiatives should be strongly promoted by governments, national and international development agencies and financial institutions.

References

Africa Renewable Energy Access Program (AFREA) (2011) Wood-based biomass energy development for Sub-Saharan Africa. Issues and approaches. The International Bank for Reconstruction and Development/The World Bank Group, Washington, D.C

African Development Bank (2017) The new deal on energy for Africa. A transformative partnership to light up and power Africa by 2025. Update of implementation. https://www.afdb.org/fileadm in/uploads/afdb/Documents/Generic-Documents/Brochure_New_Deal_2_red.pdf. Accessed 13 Dec 2017

African Development Bank (2014) Lake Turkana wind power project nominated power deal of the year in 2014. Afr Dev Bank. https://www.afdb.org/en/news-and-events/lake-turkana-wind-powe r-project-nominated-power-deal-of-the-year-in-2014-13886/. Accessed 6 Mar 2018

African Development Bank, Infrastructure Consortium for Africa, Sustainable Energy Fund Africa, UN Environment Program (2017) Atlas of Africa energy resources

Barrios Cobos S, Bertinelli L, Strobl E (2008) Trends in rainfall and economic growth in Africa: a neglected cause of the growth tragedy. In: Proceedings of the German Development Economics Conference, Zurich

Bertzky M, Kapos V, Leagnavar P, Otto M (2012) Bioenergy, REDD+ and the green economy in Africa. Nat Amp Faune 26:27–31

Bloomberg (2017) Oil giant Nigeria to sell first African Sovereign green bond. In: Bloomberg.com. https://www.bloomberg.com/news/articles/2017-12-14/top-oil-producer-pione ers-african-sovereign-green-bonds. Accessed 15 Dec 2017

Bloomberg (2016) Falling water levels hurt Sub-Sahara's Biggest Hydro Plant. Bloomberg.com. https://www.bloomberg.com/news/articles/2016-12-13/falling-water-levels-threaten-biggest-su b-saharan-hydro-plant. Accessed 19 Jun 2017

Bloomberg New Energy Finance (2016) Off-grid solar market trends report 2016. Bloom New Energy Finance. https://about.bnef.com/blog/off-grid-solar-market-trends-report-2016/. Accessed 15 Dec 2017

Bosetti V, Lubowski R, Golub A, Markandya A (2011) Linking reduced deforestation and a global carbon market: implications for clean energy technology and policy flexibility. Environ Dev Econ 16:479–505. https://doi.org/10.1017/S1355770X10000549

CNN BB (2017) How to make energy from crashing waves. CNN. https://www.cnn.com/2016/12/ 12/africa/ghana-wave-energy/index.html. Accessed 20 Apr 2018

Conway D, Dalin C, Landman WA, Osborn TJ (2017) Hydropower plans in eastern and southern Africa increase risk of concurrent climate-related electricity supply disruption. Nat Energy 2:946. https://doi.org/10.1038/s41560-017-0037-4

Critical Resource (2016) Ratings update: Lake Turkana Wind Power. Crit Resour. http://www.c-re source.com/2016/02/11/ratings-update-lake-turkana-wind-power/. Accessed 6 Mar 2018

de Strasser L (2017) Calling for nexus thinking in Africa's energy planning. FEEM working paper

Deign J (2017) Will Molten Salt Outdo batteries for grid-tied storage? In: SolarPACES. http://www. solarpaces.org/will-molten-salt-outdo-batteries-grid-tied-storage/. Accessed 16 Jan 2018

Effiom SO, Nwankwojike BN, Abam FI (2016) Economic cost evaluation on the viability of offshore wind turbine farms in Nigeria. Energy Rep 2:48–53. https://doi.org/10.1016/j.egyr.2016.03.001

ESI Africa (2016) Exploration of geothermal in the East Africa region. https://www.esi-africa.co m/magazine_articles/exploration-geothermal-east-africa-region/

Fowlie M (2017) The renewable energy auction revolution. Energy Inst Blog. https://energyathaas. wordpress.com/2017/08/07/the-renewable-energy-auction-revolution/. Accessed 15 Jan 2018

GET FiT Uganda About GET FiT. https://www.getfit-uganda.org/about-get-fit/. Accessed 16 Jan 2018

GIZ (2014) Towards sustainable modern wood energy development

Grey D (2002) Water resources and poverty in Africa: breaking the vicious circle

Industrial Minerals (2016) Grid energy storage: the next big thing for Li-ion? http://www.indmin.
    com/Article/3547870/Grid-energy-storage-The-next-big-thing-for-Li-ion.html. Accessed 7 Mar
    2018
International Energy Agency (2014) Africa energy outlook—a focus on Energy Prospects in Sub-
    Saharan Africa (World Energy Outlook Special Report)
International Energy Agency (2017) Energy access outlook (World Energy Outlook Special Report)
International Renewable Energy Agency (2013) Renewable energy auctions in developing countries
International Renewable Energy Agency (2015) Africa 2030: roadmap for a renewable energy future
International Renewable Energy Agency (2016) Innovation outlook: offshore wind. Publ.-Outlook-
    Offshore-Wind./publications/2016/Oct/Innovation-Outlook-Offshore-Wind. Accessed 18 Apr
    2018
International Renewable Energy Agency (2017a) Biofuel potential in Sub-Saharan Africa: raising
    food yields, reducing food waste and utilising residues
International Renewable Energy Agency (2017b) Renewable energy auctions. Analysing 2016
International Renewable Energy Agency (2018) Renewable power generation costs in 2017
International Rivers (2013) Development banks step up lending for hydropower, sustainability
    remains focus. Int Rivers. https://www.internationalrivers.org/resources/development-banks-ste
    p-up-lending-for-hydropower-sustainability-remains-focus-8029. Accessed 9 Jan 2018
Kamadi G (2016) Africa's largest wind farm set to power Kenya. Afr Bus Mag http://africanbusin
    essmagazine.com/N5wu3. Accessed 6 Mar 2018
Lake Turkana Wind Power LTWP project. https://ltwp.co.ke/location/. Accessed 7 Mar 2018
Levin Sources (2017) Green economy series: solar photovoltaic and energy storage in the electric
    grid
Lewis A, Estefen S, Huckerby J, Lee KS, Musial W, Pontes T, Torres-Martinez J (2011) Ocean
    energy. In: IPCC special report on renewable energy sources and climate change mitigation.
    Cambridge University Press, Cambridge, United Kingdom and New York, NY, USA
Mentis D, Hermann S, Howells M, Welsch M, Siyal SH (2015) Assessing the technical wind energy
    potential in Africa a GIS-based approach. Renew Energy 83:110–125. https://doi.org/10.1016/j.
    renene.2015.03.072
Othieno H, Awange J (2016) Energy resources in Africa. Springer, Distribution, Opportunities and
    Challenges
REN21 (2017) Global status report
Renewable Energy Science and Technology Wind Power. http://www.renewableenergyst.org/win
    d.htm. Accessed 18 Apr 2018
Reuters (2017a) Drought hits Kenyan hydroelectric output, prices set to rise. In: Reuters. http://
    www.reuters.com/article/us-kenya-electricity-prices-idUSKBN14T1GP
Reuters (2017b) Malawi hit by blackout as falling dam levels drain hydropower. In:
    Reuters. https://www.reuters.com/article/us-malawi-power/malawi-hit-by-blackout-as-falling-d
    am-levels-drain-hydropower-idUSKBN1E1197. Accessed 9 Jan 2018
Reuters (2017c) Ethiopia signs $4 billion deal to build 1,000 MW-geothermal power plants. https://
    af.reuters.com/article/africaTech/idAFL8N1OK19S. Accessed 9 Jan 2018
Richter A (2016) MiniGeo—a small-scale, off-grid geothermal power plant for remote areas. In:
    Think GeoEnergy—Geotherm. Energy News. http://www.thinkgeoenergy.com/minigeo-a-smal
    l-scale-off-grid-geothermal-power-plant-for-remote-areas/. Accessed 9 Jan 2018
Sena K (2015) Renewable Energy Projects and the Rights of Marginalised/Indigenous Communities
    in Kenya (IIWGIA—Report 21)
TFE Consulting (2017) Kenya: the world's Microgrid lab. Executive summary
Think Geo Energy (2017) Geothermal energy becoming predominant source of electricity in Kenya.
    In: Think GeoEnergy—Geotherm. Energy News. http://www.thinkgeoenergy.com/geothermal-e
    nergy-becoming-predominant-source-of-electricity-in-kenya/. Accessed 16 Jan 2018
Tiyou T (2017) The five biggest solar markets in Africa. In: Afr. LSE. http://blogs.lse.ac.uk/africa
    atlse/2017/01/18/the-five-biggest-solar-markets-in-africa/. Accessed 15 Dec 2017

Tiyou T (2016) The five biggest wind energy markets in Africa. Renew Energy Focus. http://www.renewableenergyfocus.com/view/44926/the-five-biggest-wind-energy-markets-in-africa/. Accessed 18 Dec 2017

Tsagas I (2017) What is the business case for energy storage in Africa? Renew Energy World. https://www.renewableenergyworld.com/articles/2017/11/what-is-the-business-case-for-energy-storage-in-africa.html. Accessed 19 Apr 2018

UN Environment Program (2017) Ethiopia's waste-to-energy plant is a first in Africa. UN Environ. http://www.unenvironment.org/news-and-stories/story/ethiopias-waste-energy-plant-first-africa. Accessed 9 Mar 2018

UN Industrial Development Organization (2017) Renewable energy based Minigrids: the UNIDO experience

UN Industrial Development Organization, International Center on Small Hydro Power (2016) World small hydropower development report

Waissbein O, Glemarec Y, Bayraktar H, Schmidt TS (2013) Derisking renewable energy investment. United Nations Development Programme, New York, NY

World Bank World Bank Open Data. http://data.worldbank.org/. Accessed 18 May 2017

World Bank (2016) World Bank Group suspends financing to the Inga-3 Basse Chute Technical Assistance Project. In: World Bank. http://www.worldbank.org/en/news/press-release/2016/07/25/world-bank-group-suspends-financing-to-the-inga-3-basse-chute-technical-assistance-project. Accessed 7 Mar 2018

Chapter 4
Energy Investments for Africa's Energy Transition

Abstract The challenge of bringing modern energy to everyone in Africa is a global challenge that requires substantial investments as well as a strong commitment to make the energy sector more effective and efficient within the single countries. This chapter suggests that both African governments and the plethora of foreign investors have the possibility to improve the situation, taking action respectively in terms of structural reforms (of power utilities and pro-poor subsidies) and in the coordination and streamlining of financial assistance. Notably EU countries and institutions—together with the World Bank Group the largest investor in energy development in the region—could easily reduce the bureaucracy and redundancy of existing electrification programs to achieve greater impact. In this process, the objective of universal clean cooking and the actual investments required to achieve it (particularly in LPG and bioenergy) should not be forgotten.

4.1 Electricity for All in Africa: Which Costs?

The United Nations (UN)' 2030 Agenda for Sustainable Development has set the goal of universal energy access by 2030. Considering the current status of access to electricity in the region, reaching this goal will represent a major challenge for SSA.

First of all, on the basis of which technology mix should the em-"powering" of Africa take place? To answer this question, the Royal Institute of Technology of Sweden (KTH) and the UN Department of Economic and Social Affairs (UN-DESA) have developed a unique analytical tool: the Universal Access to Electricity Model. Using open geospatial data and taking into account local characteristics, this Geographic Information Systems (GIS) model estimates the mix of technologies that will provide universal access at the lowest cost.

The model makes choices on the levelized cost of technologies calculated based on locally adjusted technical data such as distance to grid, distance to diesel sourcing, solar radiation, wind factors, water availability, among others. In granting universal access to power, the model considers grid and off-grid options, five per-capita power

© The Author(s) 2018
M. Hafner et al., *Energy in Africa*, SpringerBriefs in Energy,
https://doi.org/10.1007/978-3-319-92219-5_4

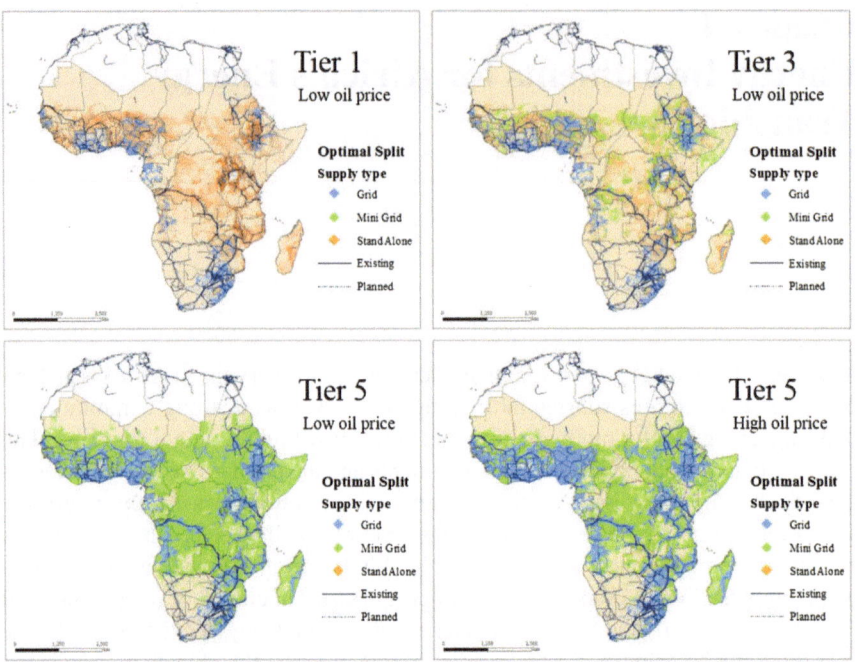

Fig. 4.1 Least cost electrification mix for low diesel cost and Tier 1 (top left), 3 (top right) and 5 (bottom left); and high diesel cost and Tier 5 (bottom right) in SSA. *Source* (Mentis et al. 2017)

consumption scenarios (Tier 1 to Tier 5)[1] and two diesel prices.[2] The model decides on the least costly option after comparing the costs of connecting to the central grid, to a mini grid, or to stand-alone solutions.

The electrification options—grid connections, mini grid and stand-alone solutions—vary from one scenario to another (Fig. 4.1). In particular, as household demand for power increases the relative proportions of grid based and mini-grid solutions increase, at the expense of stand-alone options. On the contrary, in low power demand settings decentralized generating options and stand-alone options could contribute considerably to the achievement of universal access. Reasonably, as diesel prices increase there is a shift to greater deployment of renewable mini-grids, at the expense of diesel based stand-alone and mini-grid systems (Mentis et al. 2017).

---

[1] Tier 1 provides approximately 20 kWh per household per year while Tier 5 provides 2,195 kWh. Indicatively, in Tier 1 households can only have task-lighting and recharging a cell phone or a radio; in Tier 5 households have enough electricity to enjoy general lighting and continuous use of heavy appliances, such as refrigeration, air conditioning and eventually cooking. From Tier 1 to Tier 5, scenarios increase available amounts of electricity incrementally. A household size of 5 is assumed.

[2] The model assumes two international diesel prices, 0.32 and 0.70 US$/l, used to calculate diesel costs in different localities.

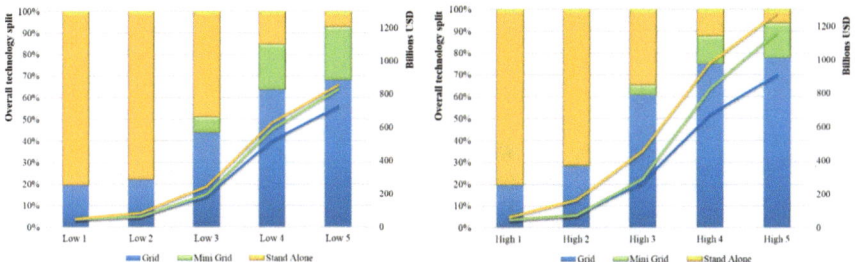

Fig. 4.2 Access split, in bars, and overall investment needs, in lines, for universal access by 2030 for low diesel costs (left); and the same (right) for high diesel costs. *Source* Mentis et al. (2017)

This seminal model is not only useful to understand how SSA's power systems can develop in the future, but it is also useful to understand the investment required in the five per-capita power consumption scenarios.

According to the model, the minimum total investment requirements to provide power to the subcontinent (with South Africa) amount to 50 billion US$ at low diesel prices and the lowest electrification level, while the maximum investment for universal access reach 1.3 trillion US$ at high diesel prices and the highest tier of electrification (Fig. 4.2).

The figure of 1.3 trillion US$ investment requirements for the subcontinent (SSA and South Africa) by 2030 for universal access to power in the highest per-capita power consumption scenario, is in line with an estimation made by Enerdata (2017) according to which around 1 trillion US$ will be needed by 2030 to expand SSA (without South Africa)'s power sector in order to ensure universal access to power by 2030.

In annual terms, this amount translates into a SSA power sector's investment requirement of around 70 billion US$ per year by 2030. Ensuring this financing will be challenging, particularly because investment in SSA energy supply remains focused for almost three-quarters on oil sector (Fig. 4.3).

Perhaps, the most striking among these historical investment trends is the one related to the power sector. In fact, although spending in the sector has increased over the last decade, annual investment in the SSA power system is currently estimated at around 8 billion US$ per year. In order to reach a good level of universal access to power by 2030, current investments need to increase ninefold. This truly represents a huge step-change.

At this point, the (literally) one-trillion-dollar question is: how to secure such vast investments? The question is clearly complex, and no silver bullet exists. However, two points seem to be essential:

(i) SSA countries should first reform their power sectors to facilitate international investments;

(ii) The international public financing made available for Africa's electrification should be better used, in order to favour the scale-up of international private investments in the sector.

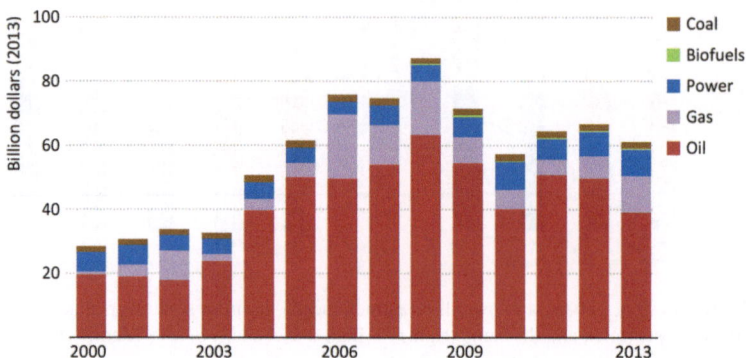

Fig. 4.3 Investment in energy supply in Sub-Saharan Africa (2000–2013). *Source* (International Energy Agency 2014)

4.2   Reforming SSA Power Sectors to Facilitate Investments

SSA countries should be the key drivers of their own energy development. They have the resources to be so, but this potential can only be unleashed by creating sufficient opportunities for investment. This challenge extends well beyond the power sector, involving a reduction of the risks arising from macroeconomic or political instability and from weak protection of contract and property rights. But it also means consistent attention to reform the way the power sector operates, in order to realise the policy ambitions of governments across SSA to improve the reliability and coverage of their power systems. In particular, two are the key reforms that SSA countries should undertake in the power sector: (i) The reform of power utilities; (ii) The reform of energy subsidies.

4.2.1   The Reform of Power Utilities

SSA power utilities have so far failed to develop flexible energy systems to provide firms with a reliable power supply and people with access to power. This is mainly the result of the fact that governments have often viewed power utilities as sites of political patronage and vehicles for corruption. Changing this situation represents a fundamental prerequisite to unleash SSA energy transformation.

Today, SSA power utilities are not financially sustainable. A seminal study by (Trimble et al. 2016) has revealed that across SSA only the utilities of two countries (i.e. Seychelles and Uganda) fully cover operational and capital expenditures (Fig. 4.4). All other SSA utilities run in quasi-fiscal deficit (i.e. defined as the difference between the actual revenue collected and the revenue required to fully recover the operating costs of production and capital depreciation), and thus need to be subsidized by the state.

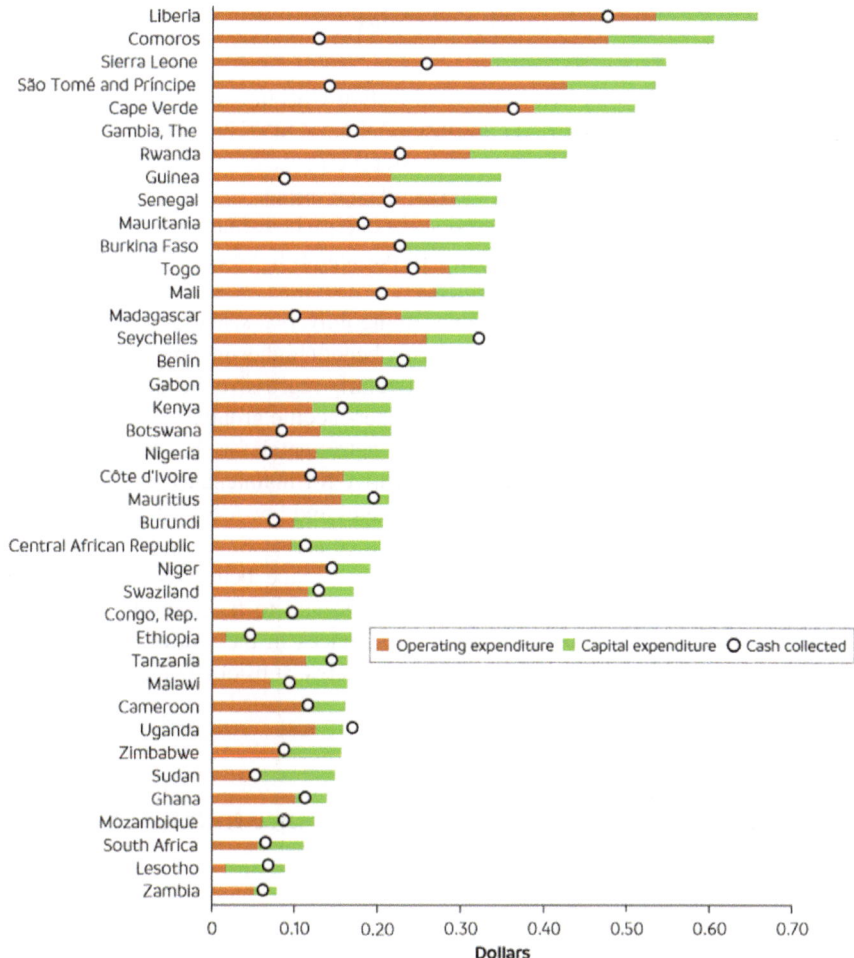

Fig. 4.4 Sub-Saharan African utilities: comparison of power supply costs with cash collected, 2014 (US$ per kWh billed). *Source* Trimble et al. (2016)

Reform is the only way to reduce these deficits and make utilities financially viable. To reach operational efficiency utilities should reduce transmission, distribution and bill collection losses, and at the same time tackle overstaffing. Then, utilities need to increase tariffs, of course starting from large- and medium-size customers, for whom affordability is not as significant a challenge as for small-consumption households. Finally, the introduction of innovative solutions, such as prepaid meters, could improve overall revenue collection.

Finally, in order to reform power utilities and ensure implementation, SSA countries should create robust and independent regulatory bodies empowered to hold utilities to account.

4.2.2   The Reform of Energy Subsidies

SSA countries spend every year around 25 billion US$ in energy subsidies (International Monetary Fund 2015). This substantial amount of budgetary resources is mainly used to subsidize inefficient and wasteful electricity utilities and, in certain cases, also to subsidize old forms of energy, like kerosene.

Redirecting these resources into productive energy investments represents a vital step in reshaping SSA's energy systems. In particular, there are two main reasons why energy subsidies should be reformed.

First, energy subsidies are inequitable. Being universal schemes rather than targeted schemes, energy subsidies in SSA mostly benefit higher-income groups, as they consume the most. Power subsidies are particularly regressive, because connection to the power grid is highly skewed toward higher-income groups.

Second, energy subsidies are profoundly detrimental for the development of energy systems. In fact, they create a disincentive for maintenance and investment in the energy sector, perpetuating energy shortages and low levels of access.

Therefore, energy subsidies should be reformed across SSA: they need to move from universal to targeted subsidies, in order to make better use of budgetary resources for pro-poor and development spending and to facilitate the expansion of electricity output. As proved by other experiences in the world—from Iran to Morocco, from Jordan to Tunisia—reforming energy subsides is challenging, but possible (International Monetary Fund 2013).

4.3   The Role of International Public Finance Initiatives for Em-powering Africa

Putting the governance of SSA's energy sector in order is the starting point for expanding the continent power systems. Without such reforms, international energy companies and investors would indeed hardly jump into SSA energy markets. This is the reason why SSA governments should act first.

However, the support of international public finance institutions will be key to ensure the progress of SSA energy transition, notably by contributing to crowd-in private investors into SSA's power markets.

In fact, the combination of political risks (e.g. corruption), commercial risks (e.g. solvability of consumers), country risk (lack of stable power market regulatory frameworks) and lack of adequate power infrastructure, prevent international private investors from scaling-up investments into SSA's power sector.

In this context, international public finance institutions have an important role to play in accompanying private investors, notably via direct financing, blended finance tools,[3] or risk-sharing mechanisms. International public finance institutions

---

[3]Blending' is a mechanism that links a grant element, provided by official development assistance (ODA), with loans from publicly owned institutions or commercial lenders.

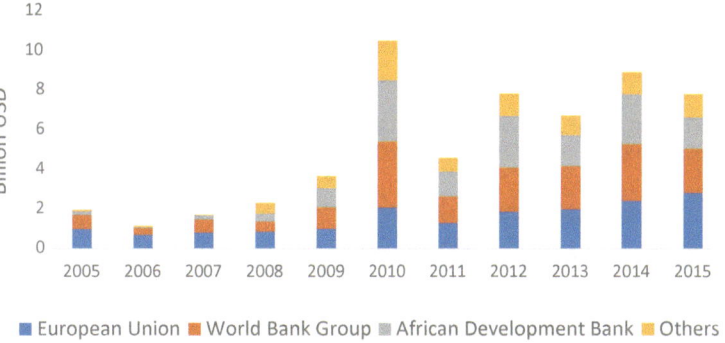

Fig. 4.5 International financial assistance to Africa's power sector, by year (2005–15). *Source* Authors' elaboration on OECD, Development Finance Database, accessed in June 2017

can indeed provide risk-mitigation and credit-enhancement tools to cover the country risk faced by international energy companies and institutional investors. This risk might change over time, as the political situation in a country evolves. Reducing the risk can enable the country to attract more investment because of lower interest rates, in effect providing an investment insurance mechanism.

As a matter of fact, international official development assistance (ODA)[4] and other official flows (OOF)[5] to the African power sector have tripled over the last decade, increasing from 2 billion US$ to 8 billion US$ in 2015 (Fig. 4.5).

The World Bank Group (WBG), the European Union (EU) (i.e. EU institutions + EU Member States) and the African Development Bank (AfDB) disbursed most of the funds in the sector, while players like the United States (US), the Climate Investment Funds (CIF), the Arab Fund for Economic and Social Development (AFESD), the OPEC Fund for International Development (OPEC-FID) and others played a far minor role (Fig. 4.6).

In terms of sectorial destination, it is interesting to outline that the WBG mainly invested in non-renewable power generation, and particularly in coal. This approach might change in the future, as the WBG announced in 2017 its decision to no longer

---

[4]ODA are defined as flows of official financing administered with the promotion of the economic development and welfare of developing countries as the main objective, and which are concessional in character with a grant element of at least 25% (using a fixed 10% rate of discount). By convention, ODA flows comprise contributions of donor government agencies, at all levels, to developing countries and to multilateral institutions. ODA receipts comprise disbursements by bilateral donors and multilateral institutions.

[5]OOF are defined as official sector transactions that do not meet ODA criteria. OOF include: grants to developing countries for representational or essentially commercial purposes; official bilateral transactions intended to promote development, but having a grant element of less than 25%; and, official bilateral transactions, whatever their grant element, that are primarily export-facilitating in purpose.

Fig. 4.6 Cumulative financial assistance to Africa's power sector, by player (2005–15). *Source* Authors' elaboration on (OECD), accessed in June 2017

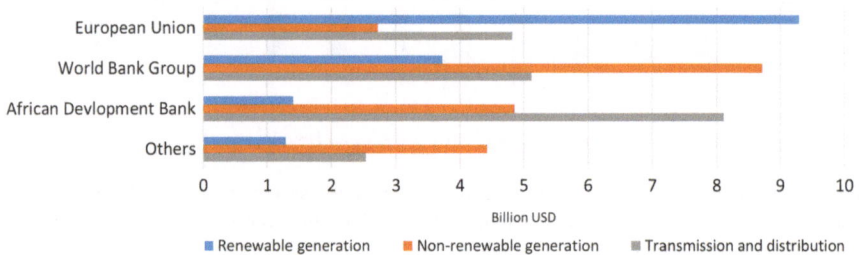

Fig. 4.7 Cumulative financial assistance to Africa's power sector, by category (2005–15). *Source* Authors' elaboration on OECD, Development Finance Database, accessed in June 2017

finance upstream oil and gas projects after 2019.[6] Meanwhile, the EU mainly invested in renewable power generation (namely hydro, wind and solar) and the AfDB mainly invested in power transmission and distribution infrastructure (Fig. 4.7).

It is also worthwhile to outline the geographical distribution of the various players' investments. For instance, over the last decade the EU was the main international public investor in North African power sector, followed by a group of players including the CIF, the AFESD, the OPEC-FID and the United Arab Emirates (UAE). The AfDB also played a significant role in the region, while the WBG was only marginally engaged there. In SSA (i.e. without South Africa), the major role was played by the WBG, by the EU and—to a lesser extent—by the AfDB. The AfDB was, on the contrary, a key player in South Africa, together with the WBG (Fig. 4.8).

This overview on international public finance assistance to Africa's power sector lacks a key player: China. In fact, the country does not disclose precise information about its development finance flows to Africa, and only unofficial estimations exist about it.[7]

However, with a seminal report published in 2016, the IEA shed light on the Chinese investments into SSA power sector (International Energy Agency 2016). The report found that Chinese companies (90% of which state-owned) were responsible for 30% of new power capacity additions in SSA between 2010 and 2015—with a total investment of around 13 US$ billion over the quinquennium.

---

[6]Only in exceptional circumstances consideration will be given to financing upstream gas in the poorest countries where there is a clear benefit in terms of energy access and the project fits within the countries' Paris Agreement commitments. See World Bank (2017).

[7]This is the case of China.aiddata.org, a collaborative online platform that seeks to make information about Chinese development finance flows to Africa more accessible and usable. The platform collects, synthetizes and standardizes data from journalists, scholars, government officials, business professionals, and local community stakeholders.

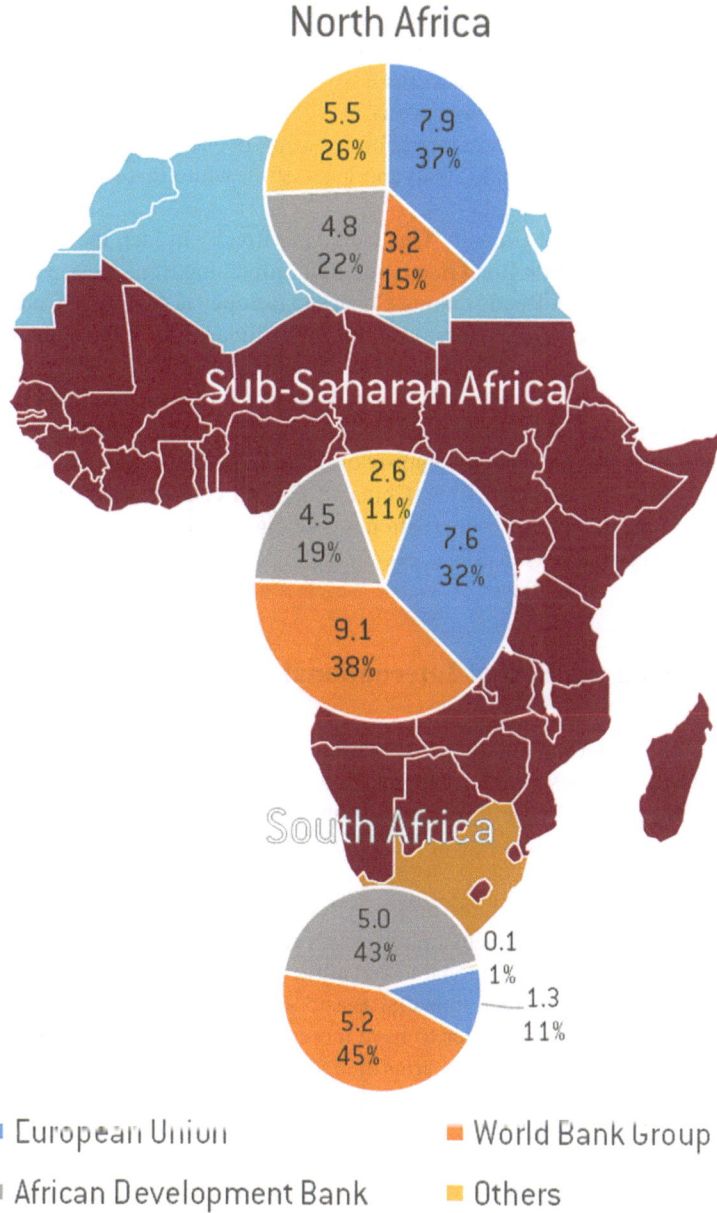

Fig. 4.8 Cumulative financial assistance to Africa power sector, by region (2005–15). *Source* Authors' elaboration on OECD, Development Finance Database, accessed in June 2017

According to the report, Chinese contractors have built or are contracted to build 17 GW of power generation capacity in SSA from 2010 to 2020, equivalent to 10% of existing installed capacity in SSA. In geographical terms, these projects are widespread across SSA, and concerns at least 37 countries out of 54. In terms of capacity size, Chinese contractors primarily focus on large projects. In terms of type of capacity, they primarily focus on traditional forms of energy like hydropower (49% of projects 2010–2020), coal (20%) and gas (19%), while involvement in modern renewables remains marginal (7%).

Africa is also part of China's "One Belt, One Road". In fact, the initiative does not only include the "Silk Road Economic Belt" stretching from Asia to Europe, but also the "Maritime Silk Road" linking China and Europe via the Indian Ocean littoral and East Africa. According to Boston University, China has invested about USD 128 billion in energy projects in "Belt and Road" countries since 2001. Of this investment, USD 4.1 billion has targeted Africa—predominantly to develop coal-fired power plants. In this initiative, China thus seem not to consider the environmental and social issues that currently prevent the majority of international financing institutions from supporting coal projects in Africa. China's focus on coal projects—alongside big hydropower projects—make international financing institutions' support for solar and wind energy projects in Africa even more important.

4.4   Making the Best of International Financial Assistance

The increasing international financial assistance to Africa's electrification certainly represents a good news for the continent. However, this is still not sufficient to bridge the gap between the 8 US$ billion factually invested every year in SSA's power sector, and the 70 US$ billion investment that would annually be needed to provide access to power to all by 2030.

As previously mentioned, the only way forward to bridge this gap is to scale-up international private investments, and for this reason domestic reforms are needed across SSA countries to create viable and attractive investment environments.

On their side, international financial assistance initiatives for Africa's electrification should also evolve, in order to have more leverage over private investors, and also over African governments in terms of incentivizing energy market reforms. With this regard, the main issue is certainly represented by coordination.

In fact, very many international initiatives are currently ongoing with the similar aim of contributing to the development of Africa's energy markets and to the improvement of access to power across the continent.

As illustrated in Table 4.1, at least 60 initiatives completely or partially devoted to the electrification of SSA can be tracked, originating from Europe, America, the Middle East and Asia.

In this labyrinthine network of initiatives, understanding who is doing what is at best challenging. As also outlined by the (Africa Progress Panel 2015), Africa's energy needs are poorly served by such a fragmented system. This because funding

Table 4.1 Global financing initiatives completely or partially focused on SSA's electrification

Name of the initiative	Responsible institution
European institutions	
The European Development Fund	Managing: EC and EIB Donors: EU Member States
Africa Energy Guarantee Fund	EIB/EC
The Electrification Financing Initiative	EC/EDFIs/US
The EU-Africa Infrastructure Trust Fund	Managing: EIB Donors: EC (via EDF) and 12 EU Member States
Africa Investment Facility	
The ACP Investment Facility	Managing: EIB Donors: EC (via EDF)
ACP-EU Energy Facility	EC and EU Member States
Africa-EU Renewable Energy Cooperation Programme	Donors: EC, Austria, Finland, Germany, The Netherlands
EU Energy Initiative Partnership Dialogue Facility	Implementing: GIZ *Donors:* EC, Austria, Finland, Germany, Italy, Sweden and The Netherlands
European countries	
Energising Development	Netherlands, Germany, Norway, United Kingdom, Switzerland, and Australia,
Energy and Environment Partnership South & East Africa	Finland, UK, Austria
Proparco	France (AFD)
Proparco FISEA: Invest and Support Fund for Businesses in Africa	France (AFD)
Sustainable Use of Natural Resources and Energy Finance	France
Danish Climate Investment Fund	Denmark
FMO Infrastructure Development Fund/Direct Investment	The Netherlands
DfID Impact Fund	UK
Energy Africa campaign	UK
Renewable Energy Performance Platform	Partners: EIB, UNEP Donor: UK
DEG—Direct Investments	Germany (KfW)
Promotional loan with PTA Bank	Germany (KfW)
Green Africa Power	UK and Norway
Nordic Climate Facility	Denmark, Finland, Iceland, Norway and Sweden

(continued)

Table 4.1 (continued)

Name of the initiative	Responsible institution
International Institutions	
Green Climate Fund	42 State Governments (via UN Convention on Climate Change)
Global Environmental Facility	UNDP, UNEP, and World Bank (39 donor countries in total)
Global Energy Efficiency and Renewable Energy Fund	EU, Germany, Norway
Sustainable Energy Fund for Africa	UN and World Bank Group *Donors*: Denmark, Italy, UK, US
African Rural Energy Enterprise Development	UN, E+Co (Clean Energy NGO)
ECOWAS Centre for Renewable Energy and Energy Efficiency	UN Industrial Development Organization, SpanisH Cooperation, Austrian Development Cooperation, EU, USAID, Brazilian Government
Africa's Renewable Energy and Access Program	World Bank Group
New Deal on Energy for Africa	African Development Bank
Energy Sector Loans	African Development Bank
Africa50	African governments, African Development Bank, institutional investors
African Renewable Energy Fund	African Development Bank, CDC, GEEREF, EIB, GEF, Sustainable Energy Fund for Africa (SEFA), West African Development Bank (BOAD), Ecowas Bank for Investment and Development (EBID), FMO, Calvert Investments, CDC Group, BIO, OeEB—the Development Bank of Austria
Carbon Initiative for Development	World Bank Group
Africa Clean Energy Corridor Initiative	19 African countries Implementing: IRENA
China-Africa Development Fund	China Development Bank and Exim Bank of China
Arab Bank for Economic Development in Africa	Member-states of the Arab League
Arab Fund	Member-states of the Arab League
Countries worldwide	
USAID Power Africa	US
U.S.-Africa Clean Energy Finance	Overseas Private Investment Corporation (OPIC) and US Trade and Development Agency (USTDA)

(continued)

Table 4.1 (continued)

Name of the initiative	Responsible institution
African Climate Technology Center	US
The Africa Renewable Energy Initiative	Partners: African Union, NEPAD, AfDB, UNEP, IRENA Donors: Germany, France, Canada, Italy, Japan, United Kingdom, US, EU, Sweden, Canada, Japan (also via existing instruments)
Climate Investment Funds Clean Technology Fund	Australia, Canada, Denmark, France, Germany, Japan, Korea, Netherlands, Norway, Spain, Sweden, Switzerland, UK, US
Strategic Climate Fund Scaling Up Renewable Energy in Low Income Countries	
Scaling Up Renewable Energy in Low Income Countries Program	Australia, Canada, Denmark, France, Germany, Japan, Korea, Netherlands, Norway, Spain, Sweden, Switzerland, UK, US
Public-private partnerships	
Energy Access Ventures Fund	EIB, CDC, FFEM, OFID, Proparco, Schneider Electric
The Global Energy Efficiency and Renewable Energy Fund	Donors: EC, German, Norway, private investors Advisor: EIB
Global Climate Partnership Fund	Denmark, IFC, Deutsche Bank, FMO, KfW, Department of Business, Energy & Industrial Strategy (BEIS), Development Bank of Austria (OeEB), responsAbility, Ärzteversorgung Westfalen-Lippe, ASN Bank
Impact Assets Emerging Markets Climate Fund	Calvert Foundation and Private Investors
Vantage GreenX Fund	South African Pension Funds
InfraCo Africa—Sub Sahara Infrastructure Fund	Private Infrastructure Development Group (PIDG), European Government
ResponsAbility—Energy Access Fund	IFC, Shell foundation, EIB
GroFin SGB Fund	Shell Foundation, Federal Republic of Germany (KfW), The Norwegian Investment Fund for Developing Countries, Norfund, and the Dutch Good Growth Fund (DGGF), GroFin Risk Capital Facility, and GroFin MENA.
Acumen Fund	Donors and international development agencies
GuarantCo	Governments (UK, NL, Swiss) KfW, FMO, SBSA, Standard Charter

(continued)

Table 4.1 (continued)

Name of the initiative	Responsible institution
DI Frontier Investment	CDC, Pension Denmark, PFA Pension, Tryg Insurance, GEEREF, Danish Investment Fund for Developing Countries, Seed Capital Assistance Facility (SCAF) funded by AfDB and UNEP
Emerging Africa Infrastructure Fund	Governments (UK, NL, Swiss), KfW, FMO, SBSA, Standard Charter, PIDG (Equity investor)
Ariya Capital Sub-Saharan Africa Cleantech Fund	USA, Sweden, Germany, Powering Agriculture, Sustainable Technology Investors, OPIC, Duke Energy
Lereko Metier Sustainable Capital fund	IFC, Lereko, FMO, DEG, South Africa PIC
Inspired Evolution Investment—Evolution One Fund	Cyane Holdings Ltd, Quantum Power, Geeref, Ifc, Finnfund, Sifem, Norfund, Afdb, Idc, Scaf
Apollo Investment Partnership ll	IDEAS Managed Fund, African Infrastructure Investment fund 2, Apollo Investment Partnership 2, cookhouse Community Trust, AFPOC
IRENA/ADFD Project Facility	Abu Dhabi Fund for Development
OPEC Fund for International Development	OPEC Members

Source Authors' elaboration

is generally transferred through overly bureaucratic delivery structures that combine high transaction costs with low impact, thus resulting in most finance to be earmarked for small-scale projects rather than sizeable programmes.

A potential way forward to make the best of global financing initiatives for SSA's electrification could thus be to establish a 'one-stop-shop' mechanism to better coordinate the actions of leading players (e.g. WBG, AfDB, EU) and, progressively, of others.

Through such a mechanism, project proposals could be treated in a more integrated and efficient way, lowering transaction costs for both applicants and financiers. Through such a mechanism, energy market reforms could also be better stimulated across SSA, for example linking operations in a certain country to the implementation of anti-corruption laws, energy utilities reforms or energy subsidy reforms. The implementation of such reforms would—in turn—allow to further attract private investments, strengthening a virtuous circle that could truly spur SSA's electrification.

Although it is recognized that such centralized mechanisms are difficult to establish and maintain, the World Bank's State of Energy Access Report (SEAR) (ESMAP), or its Global Tracking Framework (GTF) (World Bank) may offer venues for housing such a function in their future iterations.

4.5 The Role of Europe

This need for coordination is particularly urgent at EU level. In fact, as previously illustrated, the EU as a whole represents a top player in supporting Africa's electrification, alongside the WBG and the AfDB. However, EU initiatives are very fragmented, not only between various EU Member States, but also between the various EU institutions.

As illustrated in Table 4.1, part of these initiatives are promoted by the European Commission (EC), part by the European Investment Bank (EIB), part by individual EU Member States either via national promotional banks or national development agencies.

Europe's current fragmented system favors overlaps, inefficiencies and overall higher transaction costs. This European taxpayers' money would be far better spent if channelled through a unique facility, allowing policy consistency, elimination of overlaps, abatement of transaction costs and, therefore, overall higher efficiency and impact. That's it: Europe needs a one-stop-shop to make the best of its existing efforts to support SSA electrification. This can be done in 3 steps.

Step 1: Create Europe's 'EU Electrify Africa Hotspot' Starting from Coordinating EC and EIB Programs

The first step in coordinating EU's support programs for SSA electrification should be made by the EU institutions. The EC and the EIB should progressively channel existing and prospective programs related to SSA electrification into a unique box—that might be named 'EU Electrify Africa Hotspot'. In the past, a number of different programs have proliferated in this field, often without taking into consideration potential complementarities and overlaps with existing EU initiatives. There is no reason why this situation should be perpetuated. Instead of creating additional initiatives (e.g. as most recently done with the launch of the EU External Investment Plan), the EU should first put the house in order and rationalize its activities in the field. This would allow a more efficient use of European taxpayers' money, and also allow greater impact in SSA countries—due to larger scale and visibility.

Step 2: Attract EU Member States' Individual Programs into 'EU Electrify Africa Hotspot'

Once created, the bulk of the 'EU Electrify Africa Hotspot' through the coordination of EU institutions' programs will be key to attract EU Member States' individual programs into it. Clearly, this could only be done on a voluntarily basis. Member

States should therefore see a clear added value in re-addressing their funds through a joint scheme. This could arguably be the case on the basis of two main reasons:

(i)   No single EU Member State has the capability to impact alone any SSA country's electricity sector. Considering the size of the investments being made in SSA electricity sector by China and the US, Europe could only be significant by acting together.

(ii) Acting in SSA electricity sector through a joint European scheme, could allow EU Member States to reduce their own transaction costs, by exploiting synergies with other participants to the scheme.

Of course, acting together via the 'EU Electrify Africa Hotspot' should not prevent a EU Member State to do less or more, on the basis of its own political and economic preferences and priorities. The 'EU Electrify Africa Hotspot' should ultimately be seen, at this stage, as an opportunity to increase visibility and impact of established bilateral initiatives, of which Member States will continue to maintain ownership.

Step 3: Fully Leveraging the Potential of the 'EU Electrify Africa Hotspot'

But the potential of the 'EU Electrify Africa Hotspot' would be fully exploited as the various participants to the scheme will start to emit joint products. Once large-scale blended finance is available, not only larger private investments can be mobilized, but also energy sector reforms can be stimulated.

By creating joint public-private partnerships aimed at crowding-in private sector investments into SSA electricity sector—and most notably into mini- and off-grid solutions for rural electrification—EU institutions and Member States could together stimulate those energy sector reforms (e.g. reform of electricity utilities and energy subsidies) that would, in turn, further attract private investments. It is this virtuous circle that the 'EU Electrify Africa Hotspot' should ultimately seek to ignite (Tagliapietra and Bazilian 2017).

4.6   The Actual Cost of Universal Access to Clean Cooking?

The goal of universal access to clean cooking is proving particularly challenging to pursue in SSA, even more than in other developing regions, and there is a widespread feeling that the problem is not receiving enough attention, also as compared to the challenge of electrification (Energy Sector Management Assistance Program, World Bank 2014; International Energy Agency 2017; SEforALL 2017).

A variety of potential improvements from the status quo exist, more or less clean, and more or less feasible to implement, however there seems to be no silver bullet to solve the problem. Once an alternative fuel is available, habits and consumer preferences may still preserve the use of solid biomass. This phenomenon, known as "fuel stacking" (as opposed to "fuel switching"), is changing the perception of what makes a clean cooking policy successful and, as a consequence, where it makes more sense to invest to effectively tackle the problem.

So far, much of the progress registered around the world has been achieved by improving access to LPG (i.e. butane, propane), natural gas (i.e. methane), and electricity, but in terms of actual reduction of solid biomass consumption results have been mixed, particularly in the developing world, and SSA is the region where the problem remains the most pressing. As anticipated in Chap. 2, the IEA sees the following solutions to implement universal access to clean cooking in SSA by 2030, in order of potential: LPG, improved biomass (i.e. the use of stoves with a more efficient/less emitting combustion process), electricity, and natural gas. Compared to the global average, natural gas is expected to play a lesser role because of the high costs of gas distribution pipelines, and improved biomass a greater one because of the difficulties of remote communities to access or afford alternative technologies and fuels.

Estimating the cost of universal clean cooking is as challenging as—or perhaps even more than—estimating the cost of universal electrification, given the variety of possible solutions available, and possible combinations of them. When looking at past and present clean cooking policies around the world, there are also significant data gaps and inconsistencies in accounting methods that make it difficult to establish the actual costs associated to each policy.

The 2017 report "Energizing Finance" by the SE4ALL initiative offers important insights on the current situation based on a clean cooking market assessment in Bangladesh, Ethiopia, Kenya, and Nigeria. Today, most of the finance for clean cooking comes from international financing institutions, followed from a distance by public money and private investments (more foreign, less domestic). The main focus of international donors is on providing cooking devices, and particularly improved cookstoves (which is the most basic improvement). Enterprises selling clean cooking solutions (stoves and/or fuels) find it generally very hard to access financing for their business and note that clean cooking is not being given enough policy support beyond financing, even when it comes to raising awareness among consumers (SEforALL 2017).

The IEA provides a back-of-the-envelope calculation of the investments needed to solve the problem globally. They reckon that achieving universal access to clean cooking by 2030 would require approximately 62 billion US$ (i.e. 40 billion US$ more than the 20 already allocated through current policies). This equals 3 billion US$ per year, which is roughly the same amount considered in the SE4ALL report (4.4 billion US$, based on an earlier IEA estimate). This sounds like a reasonable sum, particularly if considered along the cost of achieving universal electrification, which is estimated to be around ten times more expensive (International Energy Agency 2017).

However, this estimate excludes infrastructural costs. These may be significant, particularly in SSA where the starting point is a minimal infrastructural base of ports, pipelines, rails, and even roads, and particularly for those cooking solutions that rely on ad hoc distribution networks, like natural gas, electricity, and to some extent LPG.

Let us consider the infrastructural costs associated to these three solutions. The cost of electrical cooking basically falls under the umbrella of electricity for all (see Sect. 5.1), which means that—net of the cost of electrical stoves—investing in electrification basically counts as investing in clean cooking. It should be noted that electrical cooking is a Tier 4/Tier 5 use, hence its uptake will be linked to grid expansion more than to off grid solutions. However, when it comes to natural gas, and to some extent LPG, the above cost estimate may be falling significantly short.

The present scarcity of SSA gas markets (and relative infrastructure) makes the distribution of piped natural gas to households quite problematic. In fact, residential demand is a consequence of the presence of a gas distribution network, but the construction of natural gas distribution networks in SSA is generally challenging (see Chap. 3).

Lack of supporting infrastructure is also a great barrier for LPG, which supply chain necessarily involves the presence of importing terminals (if not production i.e. refinery and/or gas processing), cylinder filling stations, pressurized storage and road distribution (World Bank et al. 2017). Clearly, the provision of clean cooking cannot be the only driver for the construction of such infrastructure, which is why internalizing their related construction cost into the cost of a clean cooking policy would result in an over-estimation. Still, the presence of infrastructure is a prerequisite to the deployment of clean cooking solution and this should be taken into account.

This leads us to a few considerations on clean cooking investments in SSA. First of all, mirroring the process of rural electrification, gas-based cooking could spread around productive uses that can guarantee a certain entity and continuity of demand. In the case of piped natural gas, these can be power production or industrial users; for LPG they can be small and medium businesses of various kind (potentially even agricultural businesses in rural areas). In SSA, like anywhere else, the future of piped natural gas will be largely tied to cities. For LPG, targeting urban and peri-urban areas first seems a sensible approach too. Investments in improving the state of roads will be necessary (though not sufficient) for the potential uptake of LPG in rural areas given the remoteness and scattered nature of settlements.

While it is not realistic to plan for natural gas development around residential uses, it is reasonable to consider clean cooking as a possible benefit from the development of domestic gas markets. This should be a further motivation for gas producing countries to consider the development of domestic markets and regional trade, as opposed to the option of extra-continental export. However, particularly in rural areas, other solutions may be more straightforward, like biogas and improved cookstoves (wood or charcoal). These solutions are associated to shorter production-consumption distances and can be easily promoted through (and simultaneously add value to) existing agricultural and fuelwood value chains.

All clean cooking solutions, from the most advanced to the most rudimentary, hold the potential to stimulate local economies. It seems therefore important to ensure access to credit for entrepreneurs and also, crucially, to maintain a vision of the value chain that investments should ultimately establish, be it LPG, bioenergy, or waste.

It is clear that governments, international financing institutions, and foreign investors, should take the issue of universal clean cooking into greater consideration. This means adopting a more systematic approach to the evaluation of clean cooking options and, as a consequence, a frank dialogue over the investments needed to achieve them. As the SE4ALL report puts it, particularly "investments in ethanol,

LPG and natural gas for cooking require long-term, industry-building perspectives" (SEforALL 2017).

Along the lines of the tool presented at the beginning of the chapter, it would be interesting to develop a cost optimization exercise for the distribution of gas-based cooking solutions in SSA, using geospatial information on distances. Given the potential synergy between electrification and clean cooking, the exercise may also reveal opportunities for infrastructure optimization.

4.7 Beyond Energy Access: The Implications of Africa's Electrification for Climate Change

Representing one of SSA's major barriers to socio-economic development, electrification certainly represents a priority to solve Africa's lack of access to energy. However, there is also another important implication of Africa's electrification: climate change.

According to the United Nations, Africa's population is set to grow more than anywhere else in the world, i.e. from 1.2 billion in 2015 to 2.5 billion in 2050. Accordingly, energy demand could also be expected to strongly grow. Getting Africa's future energy mix sustainable is thus crucial to avoid a negative impact of climate change.

For this reason, a more efficient contribution in fostering Africa's sustainable electrification should also be seen by international and European players as an important component of their overall climate change mitigation action. In particular, the role of modern bioenergy and investments in the sustainability of the forestry sector should not be forgotten, as they can significantly contribute to upscale global climate mitigation efforts.

With this regard, the potential for a new global North-South financial cooperation should also be outlined. Spare financial resources from Europe and North America could indeed be invested in 'green' assets in the global South, and notably in Africa. This would allow investors to earn higher returns, while effectively contributing to improving living conditions for the world's poorest, and to mitigating climate change. As previously stated, it is up to African countries themselves to ignite such a virtuous cycle—notably by making the key reforms necessary to create a favourable investment environment.

References

Africa Progress Panel (2015) Africa progress report 2015—Power people planet: seizing Africa's energy and climate opportunities. Geneva

Enerdata (2017) Review of the African Solar Market, Public Webinar

Energy Sector Management Assistance Program, World Bank (2014) Cooking with gas: why women in developing countries want LPG and how they can get it

ESMAP State of Energy Access Report. https://www.esmap.org/node/55528. Accessed 24 Apr 2018

International Energy Agency (2014) Africa energy outlook—A focus on energy prospects in Sub-Saharan Africa (World Energy Outlook Special Report)

International Energy Agency (2016) Boosting the power sector in Sub-Saharan Africa—China's Involvement

International Energy Agency (2017) Energy access outlook (World Energy Outlook Special Report)

International Monetary Fund (2013) Energy subsidy reform in Sub-Saharan Africa : Experiences and Lessons

International Monetary Fund (2015) How large are global energy subsidies?

Mentis D, Howells M, Rogner H, Korkovelos A, Arderne C, Zepeda Eduardo, Siyal S, Taliotis C, Bazilian M, de Roo A, Tanvez Y, Oudalov Alexandre, Scholtz E (2017) Lighting the World: the first application of an open source, spatial electrification tool (OnSSET) on Sub-Saharan Africa. Environ Res Lett 12:085003. https://doi.org/10.1088/1748-9326/aa7b29

OECD Development finance data. http://www.oecd.org/dac/financing-sustainable-development/development-finance-data/. Accessed 23 Apr 2018

SEforALL (2017) Energizing finance: scaling and refining finance in countries with large energy access gaps

Tagliapietra and Bazilian (2017) The role of international institutions in fostering sub-Saharan Africa's electrification. Columbia Center on Global Energy Policy. http://bruegel.org/wp-content/uploads/2017/09/Sub-SaharanAfricaelectrification0917FINAL.pdf

Trimble CP, Kojima M, Perez Arroyo I, Mohammadzadeh F (2016) Financial viability of electricity sectors in Sub-Saharan Africa : quasi-fiscal deficits and hidden costs. The World Bank

World Bank Global Tracking Framework—Tracking progress toward sustainable energy goals. http://gtf.esmap.org/. Accessed 24 Apr 2018

World Bank, ESMAP, SE4ALL (2017) State of electricity access report

World Bank (2017), World Bank Group announcements at one planet summit

Conclusions

Achieving universal access to modern energy is a key development challenge for African countries. While the continent somehow shares a common fate, the problem in the poorest regions is particularly pressing. After discussing some of the details of the problem, this book illustrated the variety of resources available and focused on the potential to value them for the ultimate goal of achieving universal electrification and clean cooking in the continent.

Reserves of hydrocarbons are plentiful, and even more so are renewable energy sources such as solar, wind, hydropower, and geothermal. Each country has some sort of "energy portfolio" to exploit. Achieving access to modern energy for all will certainly require considerable investments, but also a further effort in terms of policy formulation and implementation. The energy sector of most African countries lags behind when it comes to defining clear pathways to renewable energy development (e.g. legal frameworks, incentives and support to private sector development) and fossil fuel investments largely focus on production for export.

Renewable energies, which are becoming more and more competitive, will play a key role the electrification of the continent, through a mix of centralised and decentralised production. In fact, in SSA photovoltaic technology is already leading new investments in power generation including in remote areas—where it is booming as a means to provide cheap electricity far from the grid.

The consideration of a diversified power mix for the future is not only justified by economic considerations, which vary from country to country, but also by the fact that the most widespread renewable sources—solar and wind—are variable. This makes future power storage developments particularly relevant for Africa's electrification on the one hand, and underlines the strategic importance of dispatchable renewable and fossil resources on the other.

The changing role of fossil fuels in the global energy landscape forces all countries, including SSA, to consider their potential and impact in the long term. This means not only taking action in terms of air quality and the environmental

M. Hafner et al., *Energy in Africa*, SpringerBriefs in Energy, https://doi.org/10.1007/978-3-319-92219-5

impact of upstream investments, but also prioritizing investments that accelerate access to modern energy, like domestic power consumption and the provision of alternative cooking solutions to solid biomass.

Increasing access to power requires a joint action of SSA countries and the international community. On their side, SSA countries should reform the governance of their energy sectors—without this, international private investments will never materialize. At the same time, international financial assistance to Africa's electrification could be more impactful if better coordinated. This need for coordination is particularly urgent at European level, where initiatives are not only fragmented between EU Member States, but also between various EU institutions themselves.

The challenge of clean cooking is also particularly pressing and generally does not seem to receive the attention it deserves considering the costly burden of indoor air pollution, gender inequality, and environmental damage that come from the widespread reliance on solid biomass. Much more needs to be done to catalyse the necessary resources (also in terms of infrastructural investments) and political will to solve the problem.

Particularly when it comes to the development of innovative, inclusive solutions, the role of private entrepreneurs should not be underestimated. Notably, the unexpected boom of off-grid solar appliances has stemmed from the pragmatic idea of linking a pay-as-you-go business model to mobile-based payments, which allowed to make the most of the resources and instruments available. Many more successful initiatives exist, although they may not always receive much visibility, particularly when it comes to clean cooking. In this sense, improving access to credit for small businesses, investing in developing local skills, and working with women could prove particularly fruitful.

Annex: Map of African Countries and Key Socio-economic and Energy Indicators

See Fig. A.1 and Tables A.1, A.2, A.3, A.4 and A.5.

Figure A.1 Map of African countries. *Source* Author's elaboration on a map from www.africaguide.com

Table A.1 Key socioeconomic Indicators

	Population, millions	Population growth, annual %	Rural population, % of total	GDP (constant 2010 US$), billions	GDP, annual growth %	GDP per capita, PPP (current international $)	Human Development Index (scale 0–1)
	2016	2016	2016	2016	2012–2016 average	2016	2015
Algeria	40.6	1.8	29	196.0	3.4	15,013	0.745
Angola	28.8	3.4	55	103.2	3.8	6,454	0.533
Benin	10.9	2.8	56	9.1	4.9	2,168	0.485
Botswana	2.3	1.8	42	16.8	4.5	16,957	0.698
Burkina Faso	18.6	2.9	69	12.4	5.3	1,771	0.402
Burundi	10.5	3.1	88	2.3	1.8	778	0.404
Cabo Verde	0.5	1.2	34	1.9	1.5	6,551	0.648
Cameroon	23.4	2.6	45	35.1	5.2	3,609	0.518
Central African Republic	4.6	1.1	60	1.5	−4.4	699	0.352
Chad	14.5	3.1	77	12.4	3.3	1,991	0.396
Comoros	0.8	2.3	72	0.6	2.4	1,522	0.498
Congo. Dem. Rep.	78.7	3.3	57	30.5	6.9	802	0.435
Congo. Rep.	5.1	2.6	34	14.3	3.0	5,717	0.592
Cote d'Ivoire	23.7	2.5	45	36.8	9.1	3,693	0.474
Djibouti	0.9	1.6	23	1.5[a]	5.6[a]	3,343[a]	0.473
Egypt. Arab Rep.	95.7	2.0	57	260.7	3.2	11,129	0.691
Equatorial Guinea	1.2	3.8	60	15.0	−2.7	26,058	0.592
Eritrea	4.5	1.9	79	2.3[b]	0.9[b]	1,510[b]	0.420
Ethiopia	102.4	2.5	80	52.3	9.5	1,734	0.448
Gabon	2.0	2.5	13	18.9	4.3	18,103	0.697

(continued)

Table A.1 (continued)

	Population, millions	Population growth, annual %	Rural population, % of total	GDP (constant 2010 US$), billions	GDP, annual growth %	GDP per capita, PPP (current international $)	Human Development Index (scale 0–1)
	2016	2016	2016	2016	2012–2016 average	2016	2015
Gambia. The	2.0	3.0	40	1.1	3.6	1,677	0.452
Ghana	28.2	2.2	45	48.2	5.6	4,292	0.579
Guinea	12.4	2.5	62	9.1	4.7	1,966	0.414
Guinea-Bissau	1.8	2.5	50	1.1	2.9	1,609	0.424
Kenya	48.5	2.6	74	55.4	5.5	3,155	0.555
Lesotho	2.2	1.3	72	3.0	3.2	2,951	0.497
Liberia	4.6	2.5	50	1.6	3.2	813	0.427
Libya	6.3	0.9	21	28.3[b]	−7.1[b]	11,193[b]	0.716
Madagascar	24.9	2.7	64	10.4	3.2	1,506	0.512
Malawi	18.1	2.9	84	8.7	3.6	1,169	0.476
Mali	18.0	3.0	59	13.4	4.1	2,126	0.442
Mauritania	4.3	2.8	40	5.6	4.2	3,853	0.513
Mauritius	1.3	0.1	60	12.4	3.6	21,103	0.781
Morocco	35.3	1.4	39	114.8	3.2	7,857	0.647
Mozambique	28.8	2.9	67	14.9	6.4	1,217	0.418
Namibia	2.5	2.2	52	15.0	4.8	10,625	0.640
Niger	20.7	3.8	81	8.1	6.7	986	0.353
Nigeria	186.0	2.6	51	456.8	3.4	5,861	0.527
Rwanda	11.9	2.4	70	8.8	7.2	1,913	0.498
Sao Tome and Principe	0.2	2.2	34	0.3	4.5	3,237	0.574

(continued)

Table A.1 (continued)

	Population, millions	Population growth, annual %	Rural population, % of total	GDP (constant 2010 US$), billions	GDP, annual growth %	GDP per capita, PPP (current international $)	Human Development Index (scale 0–1)
	2016	2016	2016	2016	2012–2016 average	2016	2015
Senegal	15.4	2.9	56	16.8	5.0	2,566	0.494
Seychelles	0.1	1.3	46	1.3	4.8	28,384	0.782
Sierra Leone	7.4	2.2	60	3.4	5.3	1,476	0.420
Somalia	14.3	2.9	60	17.06[c]	2.4[d]	–	–
South Africa	56.0	1.3	35	419.5	1.6	13,197	0.666
South Sudan	12.2	2.9	81	8.9[a]	–9.0[a]	1,925[a]	0.418
Sudan	39.6	2.4	66	76.1	3.4	4,730	0.490
Swaziland	1.3	1.8	79	5.2	3.0	8,330	0.541
Tanzania	55.6	3.1	68	46.8	6.7	2,786	0.531
Togo	7.6	2.5	60	4.2	5.0	1,491	0.487
Tunisia	11.4	1.1	33	48.6	2.4	11,596	0.725
Uganda	41.5	3.3	84	27.5	4.5	1,819	0.493
Zambia	16.6	3.0	59	27.0	4.8	3,933	0.579
Zimbabwe	16.2	2.3	68	14.8	4.9	2,027	0.516

[a]Most recent data from 2015

[b]Most recent data from 2011 (in Libya, the civil war led to a massive reduction in oil and gas production reflected in the data)

[c]Data not available from World Bank. Estimate of GDP Purchasing Power Parity from The World Factbook. Estimate for 2017 from The World Factbook.

[d]Data not available from World Bank. Estimate for 2017 from The World Factbook.

Source HDI from UN Development Programme; all others from World Bank Development Indicators apart from the estimates of GDP of Somalia, which are taken from Central Intelligence Service "the World Factbook". All databases accessed in April 2018

Table A.2 Primary energy supply and energy use

	Primary energy supply (kilotonne of oil equivalent)								Energy use (kg of oil equivalent per capita)
	Bioenergy	Hydro	Coal and peat	Other renewables	Oil	Natural gas	Nuclear	Total	
	2015	2015	2015	2015	2015	2015	2015	2015	2014
Algeria	6	12	141	7	19,440	34,410	0	54,014	1,321
Angola	7,289	447	0	0	6,587	629	0	14,951	545
Benin	2,713	1	25	0	1,723	0	0	4,555	417
Botswana	553	0	1,035	0	1,001	0	0	2,715	1,253
Burkina Faso	–	–	–	–	–	–	–	–	–
Burundi	–	–	–	–	–	–	–	–	–
Cabo Verde	–	–	–	–	–	–	–	–	212[a]
Cameroon	5,020	436	0	0	1,921	295	0	7,794	342
Central African Republic	–	–	–	–	–	–	–	–	–
Chad	–	–	–	–	–	–	–	–	–
Comoros	–	–	–	–	–	–	–	–	64[a]
Congo, Dem. Rep.	27,252	767	0	0	902	1	0	28,887	390
Congo, Rep.	1,521	80	0	0	854	202	0	2,656	539
Cote d'Ivoire	9,395	116	0	0	1,860	1,686	0	12,984	616
Djibouti	–	–	–	–	–	–	–	–	177[a]
Egypt, Arab Rep.	1,749	1,155	355	137	39,332	36,762	0	79,395	815
Equatorial Guinea	–	–	–	–	–	–	–	–	2,121[a]
Eritrea	654	0	0	0	196	0	0	850	170[b]

(continued)

Table A.2 (continued)

	Primary energy supply (kilotonne of oil equivalent)							Total	Energy use (kg of oil equivalent per capita)
	Bioenergy	Hydro	Coal and peat	Other renewables	Oil	Natural gas	Nuclear		
	2015	2015	2015	2015	2015	2015	2015	2015	2014
Ethiopia	45,813	832	253	65	3,041	0	0	49,990	497
Gabon	3,811	79	0	0	848	307	0	5,073	2,706
Gambia, The	–	–	–	–	–	–	–	–	86[a]
Ghana	3,617	503	0	0	4,540	1,064	0	9,696	335
Guinea	–	–	–	–	–	–	–	–	–
Guinea–Bissau	–	–	–	–	–	–	–	–	66[a]
Kenya	16,208	326	349	5	4,360	0	0	25,100	513
Lesotho	–	–	–	–	–	–	–	–	10[a]
Liberia	–	–	–	–	–	–	–	–	–
Libya	152	0	0	0	11,909	5,178	0	17,246	2,880
Madagascar	–	–	–	–	–	–	–	–	–
Malawi	–	–	–	–	–	–	–	–	–
Mali	–	–	–	–	–	–	–	–	–
Mauritania	–	–	–	–	–	–	–	–	–
Mauritius	242	10	444	2	752	0	0	1,451	1,111
Morocco	1,367	162	4,444	217	11,760	1015	0	19,394	553
Mozambique	9,249	1,480	498	0	1,163	761	0	12,950	428
Namibia	237	129	2	2	1,284	0	0	1,873	762
Niger	2,213	0	65	0	618	0	0	2,964	151
Nigeria	111,566	492	29	0	12,385	14,901	0	139,373	763
Rwanda	–	–	–	–	–	–	–	–	–

(continued)

Table A.2 (continued)

	Primary energy supply (kilotonne of oil equivalent)								Energy use (kg of oil equivalent per capita)
	Bioenergy	Hydro	Coal and peat	Other renewables	Oil	Natural gas	Nuclear	Total	
	2015	2015	2015	2015	2015	2015	2015	2015	2014
Sao Tome and Principe	–	–	–	–	–	–	–	–	270[a]
Senegal	1,842	29	241	0	1,921	36	0	4,089	272
Seychelles	–	–	–	–	–	–	–	–	2411[a]
Sierra Leone	–	–	–	–	–	–	–	–	–
Somalia	–	–	–	–	–	–	–	–	–
South Africa	15,782	69	96,339	496	22,032	4,253	3,189	142,026	2,696
South Sudan	201	0	0	0	356	0	0	557	61
Sudan	9,683	724	0	0	5,263	0	0	15,670	381
Swaziland	–	–	–	–	–	–	–	–	372[a]
Tanzania	21,801	181	158	2	3,089	731	0	25,968	475
Togo	2,702	5	0	0	618	0	0	3,431	457
Tunisia	1,076	6	0	89	4,637	5,055	0	10,928	944
Uganda	–	–	–	–	–	–	–	–	–
Zambia	7,991	1121	94	0	1,072	0	0	10,243	635[c]
Zimbabwe	7,498	429	2,090	0	1,252	0	0	11,261	750[c]

[a]Most recent data from 2007
[b]Most recent data from 2011
[c]Most recent data from 2013

Source OECD database and World Bank Development Indicators, accessed in April 2018

Table A.3 Electricity production by source

	Electricity production	Sources of electricity production					
		Coal	Natural gas	Oil	Hydropower	Renewable sources	Nuclear power
	kilowatt hours billions	% of total	% of total	% of total	% of total	% of total	% of total
	2014	2014	2014	2014	2014	2014	2014
Algeria	64.2	0	97.8	1.8	0.4	0	0
Angola	9.5	0	0	46.8	53.2	0	0
Benin	0.2	0	0	99.5	0	0.5	0
Botswana	2.4	95.8	0	4.2	0	0	0
Burkina Faso	–	–	–	–	–	–	–
Burundi	–	–	–	–	–	–	–
Cameroon	6.9	0	12.9	12.8	73.2	1	0
Cabo Verde	–	–	–	–	–	–	–
Central African Republic	–	–	–	–	–	–	–
Chad	–	–	–	–	–	–	–
Comoros	–	–	–	–	–	–	–
Congo. Dem. Rep.	8.8	0	0.1	0	99.9	0	0
Congo. Rep.	1.7	0	45.3	0	54.7	0	0
Cote d'Ivoire	8.3	0	69.9	6.1	23.1	0.8	0
Djibouti	–	–	–	–	–	–	–
Egypt. Arab Rep.	171.7	0	78.7	12.2	8.1	0.9	0
Equatorial Guinea	–	–	–	–	–	–	–
Eritrea	0.4	0	0	99.5	0	0.5	0
Ethiopia	9.6	0	0	0.1	95.6	4.3	0
Gabon	2.4	0	38.9	27	33.6	0.5	0

(continued)

Table A.3 (continued)

	Electricity production	Sources of electricity production					
		Coal	Natural gas	Oil	Hydropower	Renewable sources	Nuclear power
	kilowatt hours billions	% of total	% of total	% of total	% of total	% of total	% of total
	2014	2014	2014	2014	2014	2014	2014
Gambia. The	–	–	–	–	–	–	–
Ghana	13	0	18.2	17.1	64.7	0	0
Guinea	–	–	–	–	–	–	–
Guinea–Bissau	–	–	–	–	–	–	–
Kenya	9.3	0	0	18.5	35.8	45.7	0
Lesotho	–	–	–	–	–	–	–
Liberia	–	–	–	–	–	–	–
Libya	37.7	0	53.7	46.3	0	0	0
Madagascar	–	–	–	–	–	–	–
Malawi	–	–	–	–	–	–	–
Mali	–	–	–	–	–	–	–
Mauritania	–	–	–	–	–	–	–
Mauritius	2.9	42.9	0	36.7	3.1	17.2	0
Morocco	28.7	55	19.5	13.1	5.7	6.7	0
Mozambique	17.7	0	8.8	0	91.2	0	0
Myanmar	14.2	2	35.2	0.5	62.4	0	0
Niger	0.7	71.6	0	27.8	0	0.6	0
Nigeria	30.4	0	82.4	0	17.6	0	0
Rwanda	–	–	–	–	–	–	–
Sao Tome and Principe	–	–	–	–	–	–	–

(continued)

Table A.3 (continued)

	Electricity production	Sources of electricity production					
		Coal	Natural gas	Oil	Hydropower	Renewable sources	Nuclear power
	kilowatt hours billions	% of total	% of total	% of total	% of total	% of total	% of total
	2014	2014	2014	2014	2014	2014	2014
Senegal	3.7	0	4.2	83.6	8.7	1.8	0
Seychelles	–	–	–	–	–	–	–
Sierra Leone	–	–	–	–	–	–	–
Somalia	–	–	–	–	–	–	–
South Africa	249.5	93	0	0.1	0.4	1	5.5
South Sudan	0.5	0	0	99.6	0	0.4	0
Sudan	11.4	0	0	21.7	78.3	0	0
Swaziland	–	–	–	–	–	–	–
Tanzania	6.2	0	42.2	15.5	41.6	0.6	0
Togo	0.1	0	0	12	84.5	3.5	0
Tunisia	19	0	94.2	1.8	0.3	2.8	0
Uganda	–	–	–	–	–	–	–
Zambia	14.5	0	0	2.8	97.2	0	0
Zimbabwe	10	43.9	0	0.5	54.2	1.4	0

Source World Bank Development Indicators, accessed in April 2018

Table A.4 Electricity access

	Rate of access						Population without access (million)
	National				Urban	Rural	
	2000 (%)	2005 (%)	2010 (%)	2016 (%)	2016 (%)	2016 (%)	2016 (%)
Africa	**34**	**39**	**43**	**51**	**77**	**31**	**600**
North Africa	**90**	**96**	**99**	**100**	**100**	**99**	**<1**
Algeria	98	98	99	100	100	97	<1
Egypt	94	98	100	100	100	100	–
Libya	100	100	100	100	100	99	<1
Morocco	71	88	99	99	100	97	<1
Tunisia	95	99	100	100	100	100	–
Sub–Saharan Africa	**23**	**27**	**32**	**42**	**71**	**22**	**600**
Central Africa	**10**	**15**	**21**	**25**	**50**	**5**	**98**
Cameroon	20	47	49	63	94	21	9
Central African Republic	1	2	2	3	5	1	5
Chad	2	3	4	9	32	1	13
Congo	21	23	37	43	56	16	3
Democratic Republic of the Congo	7	7	15	15	35	0	68
Equatorial Guinea	22	25	27	68	93	48	<1
Gabon	31	46	60	90	97	38	<1
East Africa	**10**	**17**	**21**	**35**	**66**	**25**	**184**
Burundi	4	5	5	10	35	7	10
Djibouti	46	48	50	42	54	1	<1
Eritrea	17	23	32	33	86	17	4
Ethiopia	5	15	23	40	85	29	61
Kenya	8	14	18	65	78	60	17
Rwanda	6	8	10	30	72	12	8
Somalia	5	9	14	16	35	4	9
South Sudan	0	0	0	1	4	0	13
Sudan	30	31	36	46	71	31	22
Uganda	4	9	9	19	23	19	33
West Africa	**33**	**37**	**42**	**52**	**80**	**28**	**175**
Nigeria	40	47	50	61	86	34	74
Benin	22	23	27	32	56	11	8
Cote d'Ivoire	50	50	59	63	88	32	9
Ghana	45	52	61	84	95	71	5
Senegal	30	35	54	64	90	44	6
Togo	9	18	28	35	74	5	5

(continued)

Table A.4 (continued)

	Rate of access				Urban	Rural	Population without access (million)
	National						
	2000 (%)	2005 (%)	2010 (%)	2016 (%)	2016 (%)	2016 (%)	2016 (%)
Burkina Faso	13	9	15	20	58	2	15
Cape Verde	59	65	70	97	100	89	<1
Gambia	18	27	35	48	66	13	1
Guinea	16	18	20	20	46	1	10
Guinea–Bissau	10	11	12	13	23	1	2
Liberia	0	1	2	12	16	3	4
Mali	12	14	17	41	83	6	11
Mauritania	15	17	19	31	47	2	3
Niger	7	8	9	11	54	0	18
Sao Tome and Principe	53	55	57	59	70	40	<1
Sierra Leone	9	11	12	9	12	6	6
South Africa	**66**	**81**	**83**	**86**	**87**	**83**	**8**
Other Southern Africa	**14**	**16**	**22**	**31**	**65**	**13**	**135**
Angola	12	17	40	35	69	6	17
Botswana	22	40	45	55	69	32	1
Comoros	30	35	40	71	89	62	<1
Lesotho	5	12	17	34	63	24	1
Madagascar	8	16	17	23	52	7	19
Malawi	5	7	9	11	49	3	16
Mauritius	100	95	99	100	100	100	–
Mozambique	7	7	15	29	57	15	21
Namibia	34	34	44	56	78	34	1
Seychelles	50	54	58	99	99	99	<1
Swaziland	25	30	35	84	90	71	<1
Tanzania	11	12	15	33	65	17	37
Zambia	12	19	19	34	67	7	11
Zimbabwe	40	36	37	34	81	11	11

Source IEA, Energy Access Outlook 2017

Table A.5 Access to clean cooking

	People without access to clean cooking				Population without access	Population relying on biomass
					(million)	
	2000 (%)	2005 (%)	2010 (%)	2015 (%)	2015 (%)	2015 (%)
Africa	**76**	**75**	**72**	**72**	**848**	**785**
North Africa	**9**	**3**	**1**	**1**	**2**	**1**
Algeria	1	1	1	–	–	–
Egypt	16	4	1	1	<1	<1
Libya	1	1	1	–	–	–
Morocco	5	5	4	3	1	1
Tunisia	7	6	2	2	<1	<1
Sub-Saharan Africa	**91**	**89**	**86**	**84**	**846**	**783**
Central Africa	**93**	**92**	**92**	**91**	**116**	**113**
Cameroon	88	83	79	77	18	17
Central African Republic	>95	>95	>95	>95	5	5
Chad	94	>95	>95	95	13	13
Congo	94	93	86	84	4	3
Democratic Republic of the Congo	>95	>95	>95	>95	75	74
Equatorial Guinea	78	78	78	77	<1	<1
Gabon	37	42	25	15	<1	<1
East Africa	**>95**	**95**	**86**	**90**	**249**	**240**
Burundi	>95	>95	>95	>95	11	11
Djibouti	>95	>95	94	94	<1	<1
Eritrea	94	93	92	90	5	4
Ethiopia	>95	>95	84	95	94	93
Kenya	>95	>95	93	86	40	34
Rwanda	>95	>95	>95	>95	12	12
Somalia	>95	>95	>95	>95	11	11
South Sudan	n.a.	n.a.	n.a.	>95	12	12
Sudan	88	81	65	65	26	26
Uganda	>95	>95	>95	>95	38	38
West Africa	**>95**	**95**	**94**	**87**	**308**	**263**
Nigeria	>95	>95	>95	94	171	128
Benin	>95	>95	94	90	10	10
Cote d'Ivoire	94	92	80	77	17	17
Ghana	90	87	88	71	20	20
Senegal	72	56	69	71	11	10
Togo	>95	>95	>95	91	7	7
Burkina Faso	>95	>95	92	87	16	16

(continued)

Table A.5 (continued)

	People without access to clean cooking				Population without access	Population relying on biomass
					(million)	
	2000 (%)	2005 (%)	2010 (%)	2015 (%)	2015 (%)	2015 (%)
Cape Verde	33	35	26	25	<1	<1
Gambia	91	91	>95	90	2	2
Guinea	>95	>95	>95	>95	12	12
Guinea-Bissau	>95	>95	>95	>95	2	2
Liberia	>95	>95	>95	>95	5	5
Mali	>95	>95	92	50	9	9
Mauritania	80	71	68	66	3	2
Niger	>95	>95	>95	>95	19	19
Sao Tome and Principe	76	77	62	40	<1	<1
Sierra Leone	>95	>95	>95	>95	6	6
South Africa	**48**	**36**	**24**	**18**	**10**	**5**
Other Southern Africa	**86**	**86**	**87**	**86**	**164**	**161**
Angola	54	55	61	61	15	15
Botswana	54	48	44	43	<1	<1
Comoros	91	>95	95	93	<1	<1
Lesotho	79	79	67	63	1	1
Madagascar	>95	>95	>95	>95	24	24
Malawi	>95	>95	>95	>95	17	17
Mauritius	7	6	3	2	<1	<1
Mozambique	>95	90	>95	95	27	26
Namibia	64	59	57	55	1	1
Seychelles	1	2	2	2	<1	<1
Swaziland	52	60	72	50	<1	<1
Tanzania	>95	>95	>95	>95	51	50
Zambia	86	84	83	87	14	14
Zimbabwe	70	70	71	71	11	11

Source IEA, Energy Access Outlook 2017